The author

Dr. Dermot Keogh is a lecturer in the Department of Modern History at University College, Cork. He has worked as a journalist with *The Irish Press,* Dublin, and with RTE, the Irish state-owned broadcasting service. He reported the funeral of Archbishop Romero for RTE.

Dr Keogh has a specialist interest in Church-State relations, having been granted a doctorate by the European University Institute, Florence, for a thesis, "Ireland, the Vatican and Catholic Europe 1919 to 1939", which forms the basis of a forthcoming book.

Dermot Keogh

ROMERO: EL SALVADOR'S MARTYR

A Study of the tragedy of El Salvador

Dominican Publications

First published (1981) by
Dominican Publications
St Saviour's
Dublin 1 Ireland

ISBN 0 907271 03 0

Cover design by Robert Ballagh

Typeset and printed by Cahill Printers Ltd.,
East Wall Road, Dublin 3.

Contents

To
the Irish Franciscans and Poor Clares of Gotera;
to
Ann, Eoin, Niall, and Aoife;
and to
the memory of Freddy Antonio Vasquez

PREFACE

"I beg you, I order you in the name of God: stop the repression."

Archbishop Oscar Romero, March 23, 1980: words addressed to the security forces during his last Sunday sermon.

The Archbishop of San Salvador, Monseñor Oscar Arnulfo Romero, was murdered as he celebrated Mass in the oratory of the Divina Providencia cancer hospital—where he resided—at 6.25 p.m. local time on March 24, 1980. It took just one shot, fired by a marksman from about thirty metres, to kill one of the most fearless Christian compaigners for human rights in Latin America. The men who organised the murder of that Nobel Prize nominee will probably never be brought to justice—certainly not in the El Salvador of the early 1980's where only the mighty and the lawless appear to be able to do as they like, not even stopping at murder and genocide.

The speculation over the real reason why Monseñor Romero "had to be silenced" may yet fill many tomes. In the following pages, I try to provide some of the answers based on research in Central America, Washington, London, Rome and Dublin. The conclusions are extremely disturbing for those who live in the West.

When the ordinary people of El Salvador, who knew the murdered archbishop so well, are asked what was the real reason behind the assassination, the usual answer may sound *simpliste* to those who do not know the history of Central America very well. He was eliminated because he loved the poor, the ordinary campe-

1

sino will say with conviction. Many are somewhat bemused that it is necessary to ask such a question. Only a stranger could be so naïve! Love of the poor is a crime in Salvador. That is the social reality in Central American countries like El Salvador, Guatemala and Honduras today.

The Provincial of the Jesuits in Central America, Fr Cesar Jerez, said that Archbishop Romero's crime was to love the poor, fight for social justice and speak the truth in public with fearless determination and disregard for his own personal safety. He was a voice for the voiceless, and that phrase has a special meaning in a country where 50% of the population is illiterate and the media are controlled by government sources and the oligarchy.

Romero could not be intimidated into silence; death held no terror for a man of such profound faith in the Resurrection. Some of his closest friends had died in violence including the Jesuit, Fr Rutilio Grande, and five other priests. The poor in Salvador, of course, continue to die anyway in a process of repression which has been termed "genocide" by one of Latin America's leading theologians, Jon Sobrino.[1]

It is the thesis of this book that Archbishop Romero was murdered in March, 1980, because his reputation had begun to spread beyond the confines of the smallest republic in Latin America; so much so that he had begun to threaten the arms life-line to the Salvadorean oligarchy and the military. Washington, or more particularly, the Pentagon was the connection point on which the rich and privileged depended to a considerable extent in Salvador for "political" survival. When Archbishop Romero wrote an open letter to President Carter calling for an arms embargo, he was snipping away at the oligarchy's umbilical cord. Then he compounded his error by urging soldiers to disobey immoral orders. Moreover, he was a source of permanent irritation to the oligarchy. The longer he lived, the greater was the possibility that he would get his point over to the U S President. The cessation of arms, military equipment and economic aid to Salvador would have been a source of great inspiration to the combined opposition.

It is the thesis of this book that the murdered archbishop held the key to future political developments in his country which threatened the vested interests of the oligarchy. And in the logic of Caiphas it was better that one man should die for the people (John, 11:49–50)

But the nation which the oligarchy wished to defend was a society based on privilege and exploitation. The Fourteen Families, as the oligarchy is referred to in the country, and the military were opposed to radical reform which would involve widespread redistribution of land to the campesinos. The loss of the archbishop has been underestimated by many Salvadoreans. A fearless voice, a leader, and a great Christian has left a legacy of solid theology behind him. But the memory of his actions and courage is poor compensation. His death has left a vacuum which will be very difficult to fill.

It was a rare privilege to be present in the cathedral of San Salvador on March 30, 1980, when the bombs went off at the funeral of Archbishop Romero. The horror of living in a country, where the doctrine of national security has such vogue, was brought home with considerable force. But that cynical exercise in pure terror directed against ordinary, poor campesinos was quite dreadful to observe at such close range. No effort was made to kill the visiting bishops. The target of the violence was the popular organisations and the ordinary poor. The sheer machiavellianism of the planned attack would have been a credit to the contorted mind of Cesare Borgia. Yet the ordinary people took the bombings and the shootings with a serenity difficult to comprehend by an outsider. There was a terrifying "normalcy" about the violence of that infamous Sunday.

In the weeks following the events of the cathedral, it was a privilege to travel in the remotest parts of this country and get to know the campesinos a lot better. What little they had in their wattle huts they were prepared to share with an outsider. They lived in a state of siege. The security forces could invade the area at any time burning and killing all before them. Yet the poor displayed pictures of Archbishop Romero prominently as an act of defiance and as a taunt to the military and national guard. Many paid with their lives for their open espousal of the archbishop's ideas.

Impressed and encouraged by what I witnessed among the campesinos on the one hand, and dejected by the brutal violence of the "security forces" and the right-wing death squads on the other, I began to write this brief history of contemporary El Salvador in the evenings and nights after spending days travelling by mule and jeep in the countryside. In coming to understand this troubled land, I have been helped enormously by the Irish Franciscan priests and St Clare nuns of Gotera. They have shared in a very intimate way the sufferings of the ordinary people. All were in the cathedral on that memorable Sunday and all behaved with considerable courage.

On one occasion, Fr Peter O'Neill had ten colones pushed into his hand at Mass in a remote country parish—a sum equivalent of a few days wages for the lowest paid—with the words which from many Salvadoreans now require no elaboration: "we saw you in the cathedral on Sunday." That phrase has taken on the meaning of "where were you in 1916?" So, to Alfred, Ciaran, Anselm, Jean, Rosemary, Gerry and Peter many thanks. There is good cause to be proud of their work.

There were also many other people who agreed to meet me and speak openly about the situation despite personal risk. The ordinary campesino I have mentioned already. It is easy to see why Monseñor Romero found them so inspiring.

A special word of thanks to theologian, Jon Sobrino, for his help in providing a penetrating analysis of Monseñor Romero's contribution as a bishop. Monseñores Rivera Damas and Urioste also spoke to me at length despite the pressures on their time from more demanding quarters. Then there were the many priests who spoke to me, in particular Fr David and Mannel. The former is on the death list and cannot live in his own parish. A girl from the Human Rights organisation, who also gave me some information, was top of the death list. There were many others, (including Juan Chacón) belonging to the popular organisations who were very cooperative.

I never met Fredy Antonio Vásquez from Chilanga, Morazan, yet his story provided me with considerable insight into the Salvadorean political process. He was murdered in a national guard barracks in January, 1980 and some research was devoted to speaking to his friends and political colleagues. His personal history is a metaphor for violence in El Salvador.[2]

I went to Salvador as a journalist, historian and a Christian. Firstly, I felt that the funeral of so important a figure as Romero ought to be covered. I went to Salvador as a historian with a specialist interest in Church-State relations. Finally, I went as a Catholic layman on pilgrimage to the shrine of a Christian martyr. The experience has changed my life, shattered my complacency and given a new personal relevance to the Christian message. The poor of Salvador can teach one so much; there the real crisis of faith does not result from materialism or undisciplined theological debate, but from the brutality, misery and exploitation of their social situation.

I would like to thank Bishop Eamonn Casey of Galway who was present in the cathedral and who acquitted himself with considerable courage; Wesley Boyd, head of news RTE who recognised the importance of the Romero funeral and facilitated the trip, and the Newsnight team—Dermot Mullane, Caroline Erskine and Lesley Mallory—who suggested I should write this book. Trocaire also made the Salvador trip possible. My thanks and admiration to the organisation which has done so much to direct Irish development aid to very heart of the human rights struggle in Central America. I would also like to thank Jimmy Galvin for the graphics and Robert Ballagh for the cover. Fr Austin Flannery and Fr Bernard Treacy did so much to improve and edit the manuscript.

I must thank Dr Deirdre McMahon who provided me with documents from the Public Records Office, London; Fr Pat Rice, who has considerable personal experience of national security ideology in practice; Fr John Sweeny, who read the manuscript and made helpful suggestions; Fr Michael O'Sullivan, chairperson of Christians for Socialism; Brian and Laura Lennon, who translated songs and poems; Miss Charlotte Wiseman of UCC for help with the typescript; and Latin American Archives and CIIR in London, for providing photographic material.

The Provincial of the Jesuits in Central America, Fr Cesar Jerez, gave me considerable help when he visited Dublin. So too did the Provincial of the Irish Franciscans, Fr David O'Reilly, and the Superior General of the Poor Clare Sisters, Sister Helen.

Finally, to Ann, Eoin, Niall, and Aoife, who tolerate my many sudden absences abroad and put up with a writer's temperament at home, *muchas gracias.*

Dermot Keogh

Chapter One

THE GOD OF THE POOR
AND THE POWER OF THE RICH

You are the God of the poor,
a human and a simple God,
The God who sweats in the street,
the God of the withered face.
That's why I speak to you,
just like my people speak,
because you are the worker God,
the labouring Christ.[1]

Leaving the plane at San Salvador, capital of the Central American state of El Salvador, I walked along a lush, red-carpetted, covered way into the antiseptic surroundings of the country's proudest showpiece, a spanking new airport built at a cost of some £3 million.

The road from the airport to the capital is quite good, and first impressions of San Salvador itself are of a modestly busy and affluent capital. The housing in the suburb of Escalon is colonial in style, and expensive. But in the newer houses no windows look out on the street, and most have high defensive walls. Many locals have begun to acquire bullet-proof landrovers imported from the US at about £50,000 a time. And the friendly looking youths who cruise around the area on cycles are vigilantes who guard the area, day and night, and have access to arms. So, the San Salvador of the trendy airport and Escalon is just one side of life in the country.

In the very heart of Escalon there is a small group of makeshift huts constructed from cardboard, mud and wattles. There people eat, sleep and procreate in one room. But this small group of *emarginatos,* whose homes

7

are dominated by the Sheraton Hotel, is just one example of the large slums of the capital which has a population of 800,000

In the capital the affluence of Escalon stands in marked contrast to the misery of the shanty towns or *turgurios* as they are known locally. And there are plenty of examples of these festering slums, held together by bits and pieces garnered from the throwaway society. The huts are built on top of each other, and hang precariously together. What happens to the people in the rainy season in such leaky hovels one can only imagine. There is no sanitation. There is no privacy.

According to statistics quoted in a British Parliamentary Delegation Report, published in 1978, some 38% of the housing in the capital consisted of tenements or shacks in the shanty towns. According to the International Labour Organisation, more than 30% of the families living within the metropolitan area of San Salvador receive less than £10 a week. The bottom 10% have an income of less than £5 a week. Unemployment runs at over 10%, but over half of those working are street vendors, paper boys, etc.[2]

In El Salvador disease and hunger are endemic. According to the Nutritional Institute of Central America and Panama, 73% of the children under five suffer from malnutrition. Infant mortality is extremely high—of every thousand babies born, sixty three do not live to be one year old. The country has the lowest calorie intake per capita in Latin America. There are fewer than three doctors for every ten thousand people.[3] And 50% of adults are illiterate.[4]

But when attention is focused on the rural sector, it is possible to begin to understand the real source of violence in the country. El Salvador has an area of about eight thousand square miles. (That's about the size of Wales or of the province of Munster.)[5] It has four million people, giving a population density of five hundred per square mile. But the land tenure system is grossly inequitable. Less than 2% of the population own

8

almost 60% of the land, while 91% own less than 22%.[6] In 1961 six families owned between them 71,923 hectares of land. In stark contrast, nearly 305,000 families were concentrated on 42,692 hectares, with nearly a third owning no land at all.[7]

The harsh lot of the *campesino* (peasant) is compounded by the kind of crops grown. Principal exports are coffee (42%), cotton (10.4%) and sugar (8.6%). Such cash crops are labour intensive. And there is always a plentiful supply of workers to snap up the seasonal employment. In such circumstances wages can be forced downwards.[8] The only recourse for many is move to the capital where a growing number of campesinos live in the shanty towns or to emigrate.

The tragedy is that El Salvador is something of a paradise with its palm-lined beaches, and its warm climate producing a plentiful supply of fruit. Inland lakes provide the ideal setting for water sports and a leisurely lifestyle. It would be possible to live in such surroundings and know as little of the poverty in the countryside and in the slums as do people in Europe. The affluence of the few is largely dependent on the poverty of the many. The popular Latin American hymn, *Yoo Soy Juan* (I'm John) states the position firmly:

> I wander like a street dog
> in my sandals from coast to coast
> while my boss enjoys the good life
> as a result of my sweat.

The message is raw and crude. But so is the reality. And the hymn is sung with great feeling in church by many Juans and Juanitas.

The poor cannot enjoy the idyllic country in which they live. Salvador is the property of an oligarchy, referred to popularly as the *Fourteen Families*. There are others, but the dominant ones are Duenos, Regalados, Mes Ayaus Hills, De Solas, Sol Milets, Guirolas, Alvarez, Melendez, Menendez Castro, Deinnigers, Quinonez, Garia Prietos, Vilanovas. All are of Spanish,

9

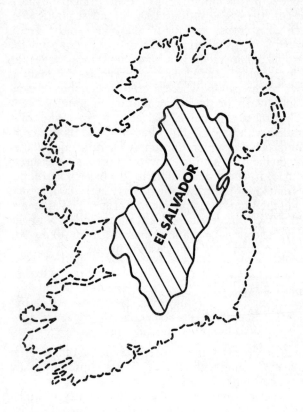

10

Dutch, and English stock. There is a small number of very wealthy families of Irish extraction.

There is no better way to get into the very heart of El Salvador than to take a bumpy jeep ride in the Department of Morazan as far as the road will take you. From there, it is a question of riding a *bestia* to your destination. But no matter how deep one penetrates, one is never really very far from the Salvadorean people. Houses are built in the most unlikely spots. They straddle rivers, are perched precariously on the sides of mountains and are miles from the nearest village or town. But it only takes a social occasion like a Mass with a few weddings, first communions and baptisms, to show how densely Salvador is populated. They come in a long file, walking for miles—the women in their colourful dresses and the men wearing technicolour shirts and carrying machetes as if they were stuck to their hands forming a sort of extended arm.

Their wattle and adobe houses are quite extraordinary. There is generally one big room with a few chairs, some makeshift furniture and a hammock or two. Naked children with distended stomachs observe the foreigner with a combination of suspicion, mistrust, interest and wonder. The first time a jeep made it up the side of a mountain along a road which was hacked out of rock and mud by the locals was a source of celebration to the men and a thing of wonder to the children. But above all, at a time of such political violence, one is struck by the sheer vulnerability of the people when faced by the sophisticated techniques of terror of the modern repressive state. One machine-gun blast and everyone inside one of those wattle huts is dead. And that is becoming commonplace in El Salvador.[9]

CAMPESINO RISING AND MASSACRE 1932

Tyranny of Coffee

Throughout, Salvadorean politics were dominated by the economics of coffee. The *grano de oro* was first planted near Santa Ana in 1838 by one Don Cirilo Guerra. By 1950, the crop accounted for 90% of the country's exports, though in 1980 it has dropped to 44% following more diversification in agriculture. France used to be the biggest consumer of Salvadorean coffee. Nowadays, the eighth largest coffee producer in the world, and the largest in Central America, Salvador exports most to Germany and the United States. The most productive Salvadorean plantations would produce between 200,000 and 1,000,000 pounds of clean coffee every year. (Some Guatemalan *latifundios* produce even more).

But the establishent of such a major industry demanded huge tracts of land under private ownership. That in turn demanded a policy of enclosure and dispossession. Between 1882 and 1912, the redistribution of land changed the entire structure of ownership in the west and centre of Salvador where the Indian population was heavily concentrated. Traditionally, the Indians held land in common under a collectivist system of tenure. But the *Ley de Extinción de Ejidos* of 1882 and the *Ley de Extinción de Communidades* of 1891 ended the practice of centuries in the departments of La Paz, Sonsonate and Ahuachapán and Cuscatlán particularly where over half the population was Indian. The new landowning class were almost entirely European.[10]

The communes were suppressed, according to the law of 1891, because they were contrary to the political and social principles on which the republic was established. Tenant farmers became day labourers on the large *fincas*. By 1920, 70% of the country's work force were

12

agricultural labourers. The farm workers lived in dreadful condition on the fincas. They were fed on tortillas (maize pancakes) and frijoles (black beans) while many drank themselves to death on the local brew called guaio. Meat and fish were luxuries seldom tasted by the *peones*.

But life was particularly hard for the Indian in the first two decades of the twentieth century. He had lost the right to communal land. His identity was threatened while the entire Indian way of life was in danger of being absorbed into an alien culture. Moreover, he was very much outside the main sphere of Salvadorean politics. In order to vote, one had to be literate. Most Indians were not. They had very strong grounds for grievance. They had been dispossessed by the patricians, the oligarchy and their supporters in the capital of San Salvador.

The British representative in San Salvador, D. J. Rodgers, was an urbane, reliable, diplomatic observer of local politics. Throughout the 1930's he made frequent reports to the Foreign Office about the plight of the Indian campesinos. He pointed out that the landowners lived extravagantly, doing little if anything to improve the conditions of their labourers who lived in miserable huts roofed with palm leaves for which, in many cases, they had to pay rent to the planters.

Sometimes the labourers are obliged to spend their small earnings at a shop belonging to the planter and I have heard of wages being paid in token checks which could only be exchanged for goods at the plantation shop. Further, some planters adopt an arrogant and insulting demeanour towards their employees and commit various offences against them and their families. It is in districts where the most unpopular planters have their estates that there is the most unrest.

Because of their financial difficulties, some planters had adopted "the unwise course of reducing the wages of their labourers. They were already low enough,"

13

commented Rodgers, "but in some cases they have been brought down to 25 centavos (about 6d) a day." And a still unwiser expedient was to cut down the food supplied to the labourers:

It is customary on all plantations to supply two meals daily consisting of beans and cakes baked with maize flour. Morning coffee is also given. The cost of these to the owner of the plantation is small, as they are usually grown on the estate. Much discontent was caused on certain plantations when the workers' food was reduced and their pay diminished.[12]

But on January 13, 1932, Rodgers reported that "communist agitation among the plantation labourers is steadily increasing in seriousness." He was convinced that this was not

a mere Labour movement aiming at an increase in wages and improvement in living conditions: the agitation is directed towards the setting up of communism with a general division of lands and property and government by the proletariat.[13]

He referred to organised groups under the leadership of foreigners. The labourers had no doubts about their programme "which consists in the slaughter of the landowners and appropriation of their lands." But he felt that the

communist revolution could still be avoided if the planters would combine to provide their workers with reasonable healthy and comfortable living conditions together with pay not lower than what they have been accustomed to. The troubles which have taken place have been mostly on the estates where the labourers are known to have been badly treated. On one of these, where about 1,500 labourers are employed, no wages, I am informed, had been paid for about eleven weeks. Also illegal counter or token currency, which could only be exchanged for goods at the shops belonging to the planter,was in use, which was another ground for grievance.[14]

An interesting picture of urban life in the country was drawn up in the early 1930's when A. R. Harris, the US military attache in Central America first arrived in San Salvador:

> One of the first things one notices . . . is the abundance of luxury motor cars driving through the streets. It seems that there are only Packards and Pierce Arrows. Nothing seems to exist between the dearest cars and the oxen cart driven by a boy in bare feet. Practically no middle class exists between the enormously wealthy and the very poor. . . . People with whom I have spoken tell me that approximately 90% of the country's wealth is in the possession of 0.5% of the population. Between thirty and forty families are owners of the entire country. They live as splendidly as kings, surrounded by crowds of servants and they send their children to be educated in Europe or in the United States and they squander money on their whims. The remainder of the population have practically nothing. I imagine that the situation in El Salvador today is similar to France before the revolution, Russia before her revolution and Mexico before hers. The situation is ripe for communism and the communists seem to have taken notice of that fact. . . . It is possible to retard a socialist or communist revolution in this country for a number of years, let's say ten or twenty, but when it happens it is going to be bloody.[15]

Major Harris was very perceptive. Genuine labour movements were to appear in the early 1920's. The Regional Federation of Salvadorean Workers (FRTS) was set up in 1923, and three years later it affiliated with the Confederation of Central American Workers which had its headquarters in Guatemala. The Salvadorean Communist Party was set up in 1925. And on May day, 1930, about eighty thousand workers marched through the capital. But the organisation of the left which enjoyed most popularity in Salvador was the Socorro Rojo International (SRI), led by Augustin Farabundo Marti.

The energetic Marti was also a founder member of the Central American Socialist Party,1925, in Guatemala. But together with two other Salvadoreans, Miguel Angel Vasques and Moises Castro y Morales, he was deported and sent back to his own country. There Marti began to work for the FRTS and quickly gained a reputation in the capital as one who could organise and argue.

But, as the labour movement began to make steady strides forward, particularly among the campesinos, the economic situation grew progressively worse. The Wall Street crash of 1929 ruined the coffee market. Exports of the crop, which brought in 96% of the country's foreign exchange, fell in value from £8m in 1928 to £2.4m in 1932.

Economic turmoil was reflected in the growing tension in Salvadorean politics. The reformist programme of President Romero Bosque wilted but not before workers had been granted an eight hour day. In the presidential election of January, 1931, Arturo Araujo came to power on the basis of fulsome and extravagant reform pledges. By December of that year he had been overthrown by General Maximiliano Hernández Martínez and thus began the country's unbroken chain of military rule which has lasted up to the present day.[16]

The tensions created by all these events led to an attempted uprising in the capital. On January 19, 1932, about five hundred men gathered in a public park and, armed with dynamite bombs, and led by "a prominent local agitator", Agustin Farabundo Marti, they prepared to march on a military barracks. When national guards arrived to disperse the crowd, Marti was arrested along with two student leaders, Mario Zapata and Alfonso Luna. The three were executed on February 1. In another incident in the capital a group got into a cavalry barracks to distribute propaganda, but were quickly ejected. The following day, an effort was made to march on another barracks in San Salvador. But it too was frustrated by the national guard. The communist rising was easily suppressed, but at the cost of considerable bloodshed.

Yet, despite the easy suppression of the feeble bid by Marti and his communist colleagues to stage a coup, Rodgers wrote to London following the declaration of martial law that the danger was far from over.

> The banks . . . bridges and . . . railways are to be blown up and the rails torn up. The telegraph and telephone offices are to be destroyed as also the local office of the fiscal representative of the foreign bond-holders. In general the adult *bourgeois* population is to be killed, after the violation of the women, and only children are to be spared, so that they can be brought up as Communists.[17]

There was an atmosphere of hysteria in the city. But the real theatre of action was not in San Salvador but in the countryside where hunger, not ideology, was the overriding factor.

Indian uprising

The economic depression, the repressive response of the coffee plantation owners to wage demands, the ousting of President Araujo, and memories of better days when land was held communally, all combined to force the mainly peasant Indian population to the west of the capital into open rebellion. On January 22 a desperate peasantry led by *caciques* (headman) took up arms to defend themselves. Few had guns; most had clubs and machetes. Unlike Marti and his comrades who looked to the future, the Indians were mainly trying to recreate the past.

They were the people whose communes had been expropriated to make way for the fincas; they were the

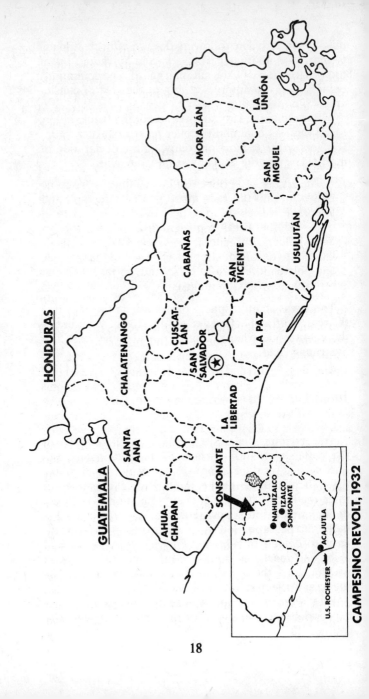

HONDURAS

GUATEMALA

MORAZÁN

LA UNIÓN

SAN MIGUEL

USULUTÁN

CABAÑAS

SAN VICENTE

CHALATENANGO

CUSCATLÁN

LA PAZ

SANTA ANA

SAN SALVADOR ★

LA LIBERTAD

AHUACHAPÁN

SONSONATE

CAMPESINO REVOLT, 1932

NAHUIZALCO
IZALCO
SONSONATE
ACAJUTLA

U.S. ROCHESTER

18

people who earned twenty five centavos a day if they were lucky, and lived in the most squalid conditions; they were the people who had seen their culture destroyed by the break up of communities. Moreover, they were the people who had to endure the brunt of the world coffee market failure. What these rebels sought was not a socialist millennium but a return to the past, to a restoration of the communal land system. Indians had not been radicalised by the philosophy of bolshevism but by the intolerable economic, social and cultural burden which the grasping coffee industry had imposed upon them.

The Indian uprising was confined to the west of the capital, and was put down within three days. In Sonsonate, between 800 and 1,000 rebels entered the town, killed the guards at the customs house, took their arms and barricaded themselves into the building. The attack coincided with the organisation of a military expedition to go to the relief of Izalco. Cars had been assembled in the main square and the attackers drove the troops back inside the barracks. Some of the Indians managed to get inside but they were shot down immediately. The following day, frightened by the appearance of government planes overhead, the rebels retreated from the Customs House and the town was again under military control.

In Ahuachapan, a provincial capital, campesinos using picks and bars atacked the barracks only to be repulsed by machine-gun fire. Rodgers commented that it was "worth remarking that the communists(*sic*) had no hesitation in attacking barracks and facing machine-gun fire with no better weapons in their hands than machetes. This determination and ferocity of the communists (*sic*) have been very conspicuous in these fights." That fact was most clearly demonstrated in Colon where the Indian Argueta, although he had "received three gunshot wounds in the body and severe machete gashes in the face, still managed to encourage his men until he collapsed dead." There were also attacks carried out on Nahuizalco, Salcoatitan and Tepecoyo. Near Tecuba, a planter called Tobias Salazar

19

was taken from his horse and killed by the rebels. In another incident, a motor car was attacked and two men were killed. The campesinos had some success against the military in Tecuba where they managed to take the barracks.

There was further violence in Santa Tecla and Izalco. Yet overall, the rising did not leave very many dead. The sociologist, Segundo Montes, found very little evidence of widespread indiscriminate killing by the Indians. In Izalco, the mayor, Miguel Call and a friend were macheted to death after they had fled from a bar, firing as they ran; in Nahuizolco Antonio Martínez died in the same way, a number were wounded while others were held prisoner in the alcaldía or mayor's office. The mayor of Juayuá was killed along with a number of guards. The much hated General Rivas died in Tacuba along with a number of others; a few guards died in the attack on Sonsonate and Sergeant Francisco Platero died during the retaking of Sonzacate. Others died in Juayúa and Tacuba while the worst incident occurred in Colón when rebels attacked a carriage, killing Dr Jacinto Colocho Bosque, Victor Durán, the chauffeur and seriously wounding the doctor's wife.

According to the journalist Méndez, who travelled around with the government troops, the campesinos did not even manage to attack Santa Tecla successfully, and they were dispersed by the troops. In Colón, only the office of the mayor was stormed in order to retrieve the machetes surrendered during the elections. A car was attacked by the crowd and a number of people were killed. There were no incidents in Santa Ana, while unsuccessful attempts were made to take over both Sonsonate and Sonzacate. The campesinos only met with success in Izalco, Nahuizalco, Juayúa and Salcoatitán. An attack on the barracks in Ahuachapán was repelled.[18] Because Mendez would be described as a semi-official source, it is likely that he has minimised the successes of the rebels.

In Juayua, according to Rodgers, the Indian leader Francisco Sanchez had controlled his men very well:

One of his first orders was that all the liquor in the bars should be poured out on to the ground, thereby preventing the intoxication of his followers. He caused all the title deeds of landed property and houses to be delivered to him and then drew up a plan of division among his own men.[19]

There was one very compelling reason why the campesinos seemed determined to attack the town halls. Besides being the local seat of a much-hated central government, the mayoral houses also contained all official documents and records as well as machetes collected before the municipal elections on January 3, 1932. Moreover, in order for a campesino to vote he had to be a registered member of a political party. There had just been an abortive rising in the capital by Martí and his followers. The government, therefore, had in its possession check-lists of all opposition voters in the country. They were likely to be used in the repression. So there was more than blind rage behind most to the Indian attacks.

Repression and massacre

The rebellion was put down with savage intensity. The officer in charge of operations in the west was José Tomás Calderón—a man who was dismissed from the army in the 1940's because of his admiration for Nazism. According to Rodgers, the general "calculated the number of communists (*sic*) there as between 70,000 and 80,000." He later declared that about 4,800 had been "disposed of" which he later explained meant that they were dispersed or arrested as well as executed.

The British envoy told of an eye-witness report from Izalco the very heart-land of the Indian population in Salvador. There, peasants were being shot in batches of sixty:

Small groups of women pass along the roads bearing white flags. Many corpses can be seen by the roadsides, which are left to be devoured by buzzards and dogs. The town is a melancholy spectacle with looted shops and houses. Volunteer guards patrol the street. The leader of the Izalco communists was an Indian named Jose Feliciano Ama. He was hanged in public in the afternoon of 28th January. He was a descendant of a line of Indian caciques and was well known for his violent character. He met his death with great stoicism and refused to give the name of those whose orders he had obeyed.[20]

Photographs from Juayuá showed houses in ruins while the inhabitants seemed to be dazed by the catastrophes they had suffered. Following the repression, it was stated that the main church wall collapsed soon after it had been used by the military as a place of execution. The wearing of Indian dress was taken as sufficient proof of guilt. Summary death was the sentence.

Miguel Mármól, the communist activist, had put the total number killed at 30,000 while Anderson estimates that only about 10,000 died. Yet another source, Dr Montes, who has done work most recently in the area states that one of the people he had interviewed—a survivor of the repression—claimed that some 7,000 had died in Izalco alone within a month of the rising. If General Calderón estimated that there were between 70,000 and 80,000 communists in the area, then it is likely that the figure of 30,000—grotesque as it may be—could well be too conservative for the actual number who died in the repression.[21]

Te Deum for the "victors"

During the troubles the clergy preached peace, fraternal love and opposition to communism. They gave spiritual assistance to the prisoners before execution. Before the outbreak of violence the Archbishop of San Salvador, Monseñor Belloso, had unsuccessfully appealed for better labour conditions. And after the suppression of the uprising he visited the president to prevail on him to stop the executions.[22]

But when Colonel Calderon retured to the capital after putting down the rebellion (which amounted to killing defenceless Indians) his victory was celebrated in the cathedral with a Te Deum.

At least one clerical voice was raised in favour of the Indians when a Dominican priest arrived at Ahuachapan with letters from the president and from the archbishop which authorised him to speak to the prisoners. Colonel Calderon, who expected a sermon admonishing the rebels, gathered the political prisoners together. To his surprise, the Dominican began:

> Brothers, you have not sinned, and you ought not to be here in the dock. In your place there ought to be the *bourgeoisie* of Ahuachapan, the owners of the ranches and the mines.[23]

The priest was ordered out of the barracks. Later the same man caused problems for the colonel when he accused him of being a theosopher like the tyrant—a reference to the president. It was only after a few days that the army could persuade the Dominican to leave the area for his own safety.

It is very doubtful if there were many clergy working among the Indians in the west at the time of the rising. Therefore first hand news of the massacres would rarely have reached the capital from secular priests and religious. But the "troublesome" Dominican who made his presence felt to Calderón hardly kept silent when he was force-marched back to San Salvador.

In retrospect it is difficult to see why such violence from the state was not vigorously condemned by the church. It is true that the archbishop did petition General Martínez to halt the mass executions. But such a private initiative was no substitute for more direct and forthright action. However just like many other Salvadoreans the clergy probably felt that the rising was the work of "red" Mexican agitators.

Like many of the well-to-do in Salvador, Rodgers had shown himself quite alarmist in the early days of the rising. He went so far as to order Commonwealth troops to land in El Salvador. Yet in his more reflective moments he overcame the temptation to see events in purely conspiratorial terms. He was convinced that the

idea of communism, in spite of optimistic declarations often heard to the contrary, has become engrained in the minds of the poorer classes, the members of whom are occasionally heard to speak naïvely of their plan to decapitate the landowners and take their land.[24]

Therefore he fell back on the conventional use of rhetoric to describe events as the "communist rising in Salvador, 1932".

Yet, on January 30, after the danger had passed away, he could write to the Foreign Office: "Most of the so-called 'communists' are merely country lads, too ignorant to know what the name means. They have been the docile tools of capitalists, politicians, and now of communist agitators." On February 12, he added in the same vein:

It was often said in Salvador, until the eve of the rising, that "there is no communism here; there is only hunger." There is some truth in this, for it cannot be said that the masses of Indians who have been utilized by the agitators have any clear notion of what the communist scheme is. They believed that there would be land and loot for all and fought blindly and bravely for that idea. They had for generations been exploited by the capitalist planters and it was now the turn of the communists to exploit them. Finally they have been shot down in hundreds and probably thousands by the Government forces. The artisan classes in the towns have probably a clearer idea of what communism is and, being able to read, are more accessible to propaganda.[25]

24

Rodgers, like many of his contemporaries, seemed well-intentioned though somewhat confused in analysing events. Although he had described the revolt and its participants as communist, he also recognised that the Indians were rebelling against intolerable economic and social conditions, and he saw the harsh conditions imposed by the landowners as the real cause of the trouble. Within the Foreign Office a very interesting minute picked up the inconsistency:

> Are we perhaps inclined to attribute more power to the communists, in such affairs as this, than they actually possess? Of course they make use of any possibilities of revolt, and revolutionaries now commonly announce themselves as communists. But these events have all the hall-marks of an agrarian revolt on the model of the Mexican revolution of 1910/12? and I gather that all the elements which result in such revolts were present in an aggravated form. The Mexican revolution, if it had taken place after that in Russia would no doubt have taken a communist form, or at any rate have used communist labels. If a permenent cure is to be found in Salvador, it will probably have to be in the direction of a removal of the abuses in the land system (which I gather from his paper are serious) rather than in the suppression of communist theories—however desirable that may be.[26]

In January, 1932, there were really two uprisings —one in the capital led by Martí which was as unsuccessful as it was ineptly led; and the other in the countryside led by Indian *caciques* (headmen). The former sought the establishment of Soviets in Salvador and looked to the future, while the Indians looked back for their objectives to a time when land was held in common and their culture and language were vibrant. There were comparatively few casualties in San Salvador. In the countryside, over 30,000 Indians probably died. Their culture had been destroyed, many were afraid even to wear Indian dress and they were thereafter to be denied the right to join a trade union. Under successive military rulers, life was to become harsher for the Indian.[27]

THE REIGN OF THE MEN ON HORSEBACK

The Salvadoreans have had to live with violence for centuries. Originally, the country was inhabited by Mayans and Pipils. But in 1524, Pedro de Alvarado occupied the capital Cuscatlan for the Spaniards. San Salvador was founded the following year. Together with neighbouring Sonsonate, both developed as separate provinces under the Audiencia of Guatemala. In 1786, Salvador was given the status of an intendancy, still subordinate to the Spaniards.

Fr Jose Matias Delgado, later the first bishop of San Salvador, led a rising against the Spaniards in 1811. When Guatemala broke with Spain in 1828, San Salvador remained within a Central American Federation. But with the breakup of that grouping in 1841, Salvador won full independence. There followed a period of considerable political instability with coup provoking counter-coup, as two rival groups of powerful coffee-plantation creoles—"Liberals" and "Conservatives" —jockeyed with each other for control. The situation remained politically confused well into the 1920's. The oligarchy, backed by the military, maintained control of the country. British and American capital stimulated economic development.

General Martinez, who gained power in the coup of 1931, was known as "el Brujo" because of his fond attachment to magic. He remained in power for thirteen years—an example of political longevity uncommon in Salvadorean history. His regime collapsed in 1944 in the wake of a general strike. There followed a series of soldier politicians who ran the country with little emphasis on reform. The most significant of these militarymen was Major Oscar Osorio who was "elected" president in 1950 and remained in office for a full term of six years. In this period, the country enjoyed considerable economic prosperity. Osorio founded the *Partido Revolucionario de Unificacion Democratica* (PRUD) which dominated Salvadorean political life for the next ten years. Then in 1956 Colonel Jose Maria Lemus became president and remained in power by keeping political opponents in jail. He visited the United States in March, 1959, and was received by President Eisenhower before taking part in a ticker-tape parade in Manhattan. He returned to a country where the political opposition was beginning to show more open hostility to the regime. All political rallies were banned in September, 1960. Troops invaded the university, systematically smashing up offices, classrooms, and laboratories and beating students. The response from the students was a mass street demonstration which resulted in bloodshed when troops were ordered to open fire to disperse the crowds.

The violence provoked a reaction from the moderates within the army. Colonel Cesar Yanez Urias overthrew the government, dissolved Congress and set up a six-man junta with promises of free elections, by 1962. The putsch was made up of a few young progressive officers who had connections with the leaders of a leftwing movement known as PRAN. American reaction to the new progressive junta was divided. According to one source, the State Department refused to recognise the new government on the advice of Ambassador Thorsten Kalijarvi who branded the officers as pro-Cuban. In the four months which followed the coup, PRAN leaders made it clear that they were pro-Castro. As a result, the young officers who led the revolt were disowned by the army chief of staff although it was clear at the time that they were not *castroites* pure and simple. The junta was replaced by a civilian and military ruling council on January 15, 1961. Its strongman was Colonel Julio Adalberto Rivera. And the Kennedy administration gave it full backing, on condition that it initiate a programme of reforms. The State Department was trying to court some of the more progressive elements in the military and the universities without encouragting radicalism. It was a ploy which brought them into direct conflict with the strong American lobby backing the Fourteen Families.

The measures proposed by the council were but slight reforms in relation to the enormous social problems of the country, but they were sufficient to alarm the oligarchy.

Decrees were issued stating that farm and industrial workers had to be paid for Sundays off, rent was to be reduced by 30% and, most revolutionary of all, the central bank was to be nationalised, and strict currency controls established to prevent the outflow of capital. The response from the wealthy was quite unpatriotic, and there was a flight of money from the country into Swiss and American banks.

But the coffee lobby would not accept the reforms. Influence was used in the United States to pressurise the Kennedy administration into urging the Council to call early general elections. There was the argument that in a country where the coup and not elections brought governments to power, the council set up by the last putsch was *illegal*.

The Council then began a more rapid programme of reform. Colonel Rivera resigned office and formed the National Conciliation Party (PGN) to fight on a "progressive" ticket, in the election for a new constituent assembly. There were 800,000 registered voters and seven opposition parties. But amid cries of fraud, Rivera's party won all 54 seats. As a result the opposition refused to participate in the presidential election which was held in April, 1962. Not surprisingly, Rivera was elected.

That same year a new constitution was introduced which proved to be one of the most liberal in Latin America. It made provision for presidential elections every five years and for elections to a one-chamber legislative assembly; and municipal elections every two years. In 1963, proportional representation was introduced. But such paper reforms did little to change the political power structure. Rivera was succeeded by another officer, Colonel Fidel Sanchez Hernandez, when his term of office ended in 1967.[28]

Electoral Fraud

But the opposition groupings had become more efficient. The Christian Democratic Party (PDC) had been founded in 1960, and by the end of the decade was being led by Jose Napoleon Duarte—then a popular mayor of Salvador. He advocated a reform programme similar to that of Dr Eduardo Frei in Chile. But, because of persistent electoral frauds, by 1968 the Christian Democrats still only had 15 seats in the 54-strong national assembly. Two other constitutional parties had, among others been founded in the 1960's, the National Revolutionary Party in 1967 and the National Democratic Union in 1969. All three formed the broadly based electoral coalition of the United National Opposition (ONU) in 1971 to fight the presidential election in the following year. But in flagrant violation of popular opinion, Colonel Arturo Armando Molina—the military heir apparent—"defeated" Jose Napoleon Duarte by open electoral fraud, intimidation and bloodshed. The 1977 election was the final attempt by the opposition to try to participate in the "constitutional" system of the Salvadorean democracy. But the experience of 1972 was repeated, and a General Carlos Humberto Romero was declared winner against a combined opposition candidate amid cries of fraud which resulted in huge protests that were savagely repressed.

According to official results, which were announced on February 24, General Romero got 812,281 votes while Colonel Ernesto Claramount, a retied career officer candidate for the Unión Nacional Opositora (UNO), received 394,661. The electorate was roughly

1,800,000 out of a total population of over 4,000,000. The slogan under which General Romero campaigned, "democracy or communism", had triumphed, or had it? Cries of massive electoral fraud were heard immediately from UNO supporters. It was claimed that 400,000 bogus names had been put on the electoral list. According to Keesing's, press reports put the fraud at 150,000—"there being 600,000 more voters than on the 1972 lists, only 450,000 of whom could, according to the census figures, be accounted for as newly-eligible voters." There were also claims, which could be substantiated, that ballot boxes had been stuffed with pro-Romero votes, while UNO observers were only allowed to be at 1,000 of the 3,500 polling stations. There were also charges of intimidation and violence against the opposition.

In an effort to draw intenational attention to the fraudulent nature of the elections, UNO supporters occupied the main square in the capital on February 21. Shops were closed, public transport halted by a general strike and barricades were erected in the suburbs of the capital. A week later, the demonstrators were evacuated. And the UNO vice presidential candidate Antonio Morales Erlich, went into the safety of the Costa Rican embassy with other prominent UNO members. The government declared a state of siege. On March 1, 1977 the central electoral council officially confirmed General Romero as president. The decision was a very severe blow for Salvadorean democracy.

In the congressional and municipal election of 1978, the combined opposition refused to participate and the government "resurrected the Popular Salvadorean Party (PPS), a minor rightwing party, to preserve some semblance of democracy".[29]

But the constant disappointment with participation in fraudulent elections had given rise to a number of popular organisations, The Bloque Popular Revolucionario (BPR) with its military wing, the Fuerzas Populares de Liberación, being the strongest. The political section is led by Juan Chacón. FAPU, Frente de Acion

Popular Unificada, is also very strong, and has a guer-rilla wing called FARN, Fuerzas Armadas de la Resis-tencia Nacional. The last of the three largest popular organisations is Ligas Populares de 28 de Febrero (LP 28) with an armed wing, Ejercito Revolucionario del Pueblo, ERP.[30] Among the *campesinos,* two strong clandestine associations developed, the Christian Fed-eration of Campesinos (FECCAS) and the Union of Rural Workers (UTC) both with very strong backing from the younger clergy.[31]

Law and ORDEN

While the initiative seemed to be passing to the pop-ular orgnisations there was a determined effort to arrest the process by the use of the most draconian tactics on the part of the government. Repression was very intense. And President Romero was aided in his efforts by a number of rightwing para-military organisations.

ORDEN had been established in the late 1960's to help the government control "subversion" in the coun-tryside. It was a civilian group which rose in strength to between 40,000 and 60,000.[32] Members had their own special card which bestowed its own privileges; they were not harassed at checkpoints, and in return for information they could enjoy other perks. But some acted as more than just the eyes and ears of the regime. They participated in the raids on villages and were responsible for quite a number of summary executions. But despite the lawlessness of this movement, it received a subsidy directly from the government. President Rom-ero told a visiting Amnesty International team quite freely in 1978 that ORDEN had "government support and acts in coordination with government activities aimed at combatting terrorism." The government would only consider disbanding that group when the "situation changes" and "when people in the cities and in the country feel secure and tranquil . . . then and only then can consideration be given to dissolving ORDEN." A large staff, with a monthly budget of 22,000 colones (£4,400), operated from the Presidential Palace.

If ORDEN operated as an auxiliary group to the security forces, there were other even more sinister groups who killed victims with impunity. The Union Guerrera Blanca (UGB), the Movimiento Anticomunista Nacional Organizado and the Esquadron de la Muerte are among some of the more prominent paramilitary rightwing groups operating in the country.

Without the help of ORDEN, the armed forces would be entirely over-stretched. The army is estimated to be over 6,000-strong; the navy has just over 200 men while the airforce has over 1,000. The national guard numbers 2,500 and an organised reserve called the Territorial Service is believed to be over 75,000. The 1962 constitution—the fourteenth since the country became independent in 1841—declares the army to be a professional apolitical group controlled by a national assembly. But since the army has been virtually in power without a break since 1931, this point is slightly academic.

In the past, the Salvadorean army has been trained by the Chileans, and the ties between these two Latin American countries remained quite strong until after World War II when the United States took over the teaching role. Aid came through the Military Assistance Programme. In 1970 the United States mantained both army and air force training missions in the country, "and a close working relationship existed between both services."[33] There was, therefore, "a shift in focus leading to the adoption of United States procedures and doctrines."[34]

The Salvadorean army has only twice seen action this century; the first time was the brief war with Guatemala in 1906, and the second occurred in 1969 during the "soccer war" with Honduras. For the rest of the time, the military have been involved in maintaining internal "order". The coup which overthrew the leftist military junta of October 26, 1960, issued a proclamation on January 25, 1961, signalling a very important ideological change in the self-perceived role of the armed forces. The military no longer guaranteed to protect the constitution, they sought to govern too.

Throughout the remainder of the 1960's, the armed forces began to expand their hold on government. They were no longer satisfied with such conventional ministries as defence. In the cabinet of General Fidel Sánchez Hernández (1968–1972), officers held the posts of Defence, Labour, two junior ministries—Defence and Agriculture—and the private secretaryship to the President of the Republic. But in the regime of General Carlos Humberto Romero (1977—1978), the military held Defence, Labour, Foreign Affairs, and the Interior coupled with the junior ministry of Defence and other minor posts. Besides the greater military presence in government, there was also quite an expansion in the public and private sectors.[35]

Moreover, the military institution had become much more dependent on America for "procedures and doctrines" according to semi-official US sources. In practical terms, that meant more Salvadorean officers were going abroad for training. Between 1968 and 1973, one hundred and eighty one security force personnel attended courses outside the country; of these one hundred and twelve went to Panama, thirty five to the USA and seven to Mexico while three went to Taiwan. These numbers, of course, take no account of the Salvadoreans trained and armed in their own country by Pentagon personnel under the Military Assistance Programme.

In the 1960's and 1970's, a succession of democratic regimes in Latin America fell under the influence of military juntas with a common ideology born, in part, from the similarity of their training. In 1964, Goulart was overthrown in Brazil and replaced by a strongly authoritarian government. In 1973, two of Latin America's model democracies—Chile and Uruguay—fell to the men on horseback. Argentina joined the club in 1976.

The National security state

What Salvadoreans witnessed in the 1960's and 1970's was the emergence of that phenomenon known as the national security state, a political concept explored most ably by the Belgian priest and missionary José Comblin.[36] The latter traces the origins of the authoritarian ideology in Latin America from the years after the second world war when the United States set up the Central Intelligence Agency and the National Security Council (NSC). Several Latin American countries followed the example of Washington. Unlike the United States, however, where Congress acted as a democratic brake on CIA activities, Bolivia, Brazil, Argentina, Chile, Uruguay, Guatemala and El Salvador have all followed that example and taken the national security ideology "to its logical conclusions with devastating results."[37]

The military have developed their own philosophy based on the belief that civilian governments in succession betrayed their countries through incompetent, corrupt, ineffectual, soft-headed administration. They speak of the need for national regeneration in the name of science, democracy and Christianity before power can be returned to a chastened elite. The process should minimise the power of the masses who are "sluggish, stupid and passive" ever liable "to be 'conned' by demogogues or fall victim to infiltration by subversives."[38] There is also a fundamental corporatism associated with the national security ideology: every aspect of national life and every activity of the citizen will be energised towards protecting the nation. There is therefore the need to develop institutions which will "protect" the homeland.

Logically, the fusion of defence and internal security means that the secret services are sovereign and outside the jurisdiction of the courts. Necessity makes its own laws. The greater the "threat" to security, the more ruthless the secret service may become in its treatment of political prisoners.

In another place, Comblin sets out the characteristics of the national security doctrine as conceptual rigour, inflexibility, and abstract rationalism, where everything is derived in a totally deductive fashion from the postulate of total war:

> The entire society is submitted to the implacable logic of military stratregy, whose principles are assumed to be extendable to the totality of human reality; society is transformed into a military camp and submitted to the rigid codes of military quarters—a society in barracks. That the alleged end of this integration will be the salvation of freedom and democracy may be considered by many as an insufficient compensation; in a world of total war they fear they won't live long enough to see the dawn of the promised era.[39]

Most Latin American coups are conducted in the name of democracy and Christianity. Moreover, the generals and the oligarchs are rarely aware of any contradiction between the national security ideology and the teachings of the Gospel. The rhetoric of the right makes considerable play of the threat from communism and subversion. A more discerning Christian attitude towards political opposition is viewed with considerable hostility. Coupled with that, the political language of the military is often revivalist and fundamentalist in tone. There is a contrived identity of purpose between the church and the nation. And this is most easily achieved by quoting from late nineteenth century encyclicals, placing them in a false context. In return for co-operation, the church is offered a number of privileges and inducements: the development of a strongly religious educational system, censorship of books contrary to church teaching, close co-operation between church and state symbolised by the strong military presence at religious events.

The bargain or pact has proved to be very seductive. Many Catholics have accepted the opportunity to "control" the future through an alliance with the military. In

Salvador, ORDEN with its approximately sixty thousand members, has always been strongly represented in the congregations for liturgical celebrations.

There is a strange dichotomy in Salvadorean public life between the practice of the national security philosophy and the liberal nature of the constitution.[40] That has set up a considerable tension in certain quarters; there was a healthy antagonism to the banalities of rightwing conspiracy theorists. There was an awareness of the blatant contradictions between constitutional guarantees and the practice of law and ORDEN. There were those who considered that General Romero ought not to be allowed continue along his manic way to "total war". The US State Department also favoured a new departure in Salvador.[41]

Military coup, 1979: hope and despair

The growing hegemony of the national security ideology threatened Salvadoreans with an apocalypse under the regime of President Romero. In the summer of 1979 there was talk of a Saint Bartholomew's Day solution to the country's political problems—massacre all "opponents" of the regime. The constitution of 1962 upheld the sovereignty of the Salvadorean people. The reality was quite different. Defence of the nation had replaced respect for the democratic rights of citizens. About six hundred people had been assassinated or joined the list of "missing persons" that year. Many were subjected to cruel, inhuman and degrading treatment by the security forces. One of the most publicised cases of torture concerned Apolinario Baires, who died on March 4, 1979 from burns after being detained by the National Guard.[42]

Many other cases of brutality were proven against the security forces, such that the British Labour government was prompted early in 1977 to cancel a contract worth nearly £1 million for the supply of armoured cars to El Salvador.

Meanwhile the popular organisations were growing in strength as people became disillusioned with traditional politics. The BPR, FAPU and LP28 are reported to have reached strengths of sixty thousand, thirty thousand, and ten thousand respectively. And their military wings, ERP, FPL, and FARN had an estimated two thousand activists under arms.

Throughout this period, leftwing activity added to the terror in the country. The FPL kidnapped the Foreign Minister, Borgonovo Pohl (aged 38) on April 19, 1977. When the government refused to release thirty seven prisoners, the body of the politician, who came from one of the country's wealthiest families, was found in Santa Tecla, on May 11. On November 10, 1977, the Ministry of Labour was occupied by the BPR. In the following year, kidnappings, murders, and repression continued. Two British executives of the Bank of London and South America (a Lloyds subsidiary) were kidnapped and released months later for a reported ransom of £4 million. Embassies were occupied. The Minister for Education was murdered. President Romero declared a state of siege.

Then on May 8, 1979, television viewers around the world saw the national guard open fire with automatic weapons on a crowd clambering up the steps of the cathedral. Horrified viewers saw people being shot in front of their very eyes. Twenty three people died and over seventy were wounded. The security forces had opened fire first. General Romero blamed the violence on "international subversion". Another state of siege followed further occupations of embassies. On May 17, President Romero had called on television for a national dialogue with the moderate opposition but he excluded the BPR. But the offer was not taken up by the moderates.

In August, 1979, President Romero made an attempt at reform, intimating that free elections would be held sometime in 1980, supervised by the Organisaton of American States. A general amnesty was declared, and the Red Cross was asked to inspect the prisons. A

National Dialogue Body was set up. But these proposals drew approval only from official state groups. For one thing, the memory of fraud at the polls left most of the opposition deeply suspicious of the promised free elections. While the government and the military seemed to be moving into deeper disarray, the Popular Organisations felt compelled to set up a Popular Forum in September. The main opposition groups all took part.

But in July, 1979, Central America was hit by a political earthquake: On the 17th, the Nicaraguan dictator, Somoza, fled the country and went into exile in Florida where he promptly accused Cuba of complicity in the overthrow of his regime. But in the capital, Managua, the Sandinistas had taken over causing a very high reading on the political seismographs of most Central American dictatorships. Salvador, which is separated by a short sea journey from Nicaragua, reacted strongly to the leftwing guerrilla victory.[43]

It is probably true that, had the Americans wanted, they could have propped Somoza up indefinitely. But the new Carter line on Latin America had begun to make itself felt in the depleted arsenals of repressive regimes. However, there remained a strong contradiction in interest between the White House and the Pentagon. A foreign policy reflecting a concern for human rights had very serious military repercussions. Nicaragua was an example of what would happen if emphasis was taken off US strategic and economic interest. An editorial in the *Economist* summed up a section of feeling in the US:

> Just 600 miles south of the United States lies an isthmus where politics has scarcely changed since the plunderers of imperial Spain stepped ashore 450 years ago. Ever since, most of the tiny, fertile, earthquake-prone republics of central America have been lorded over by a small number of the very rich, protected by casually cruel soldiers. Successive governments of the United States have kept their eyes averted from the picturesque ex-colonial slum down

38

the road. Now the slum is seething. Nicaragua's dictatorship has been burnt down. El Salvador's is threatening to burst into communist flames. Guatemala, Honduras and possibly Panama and Costa Rica too, are threatened with savage repression by their armies. The casualty list alone calls for more attention than the post-Afghan world has been able to spare.[44]

But the *Economist* advised that to avoid a Marxist takeover, the ruling army should use the pauses between revolutionary attacks to hand power over to civilian reformists. The latter would dilute the power of the army's friends but "they will not march them to the gallows." With the lesson of Nicaragua firmly in mind, the Carter administration pushed for an *Economist*-style solution in Salvador. They met with a ready response from elements within the army free of the doctrine of national security. The apolitical professionalism of the Salvadorean officer class had survived in part. On the other hand, there was a feeling that, unless something was done immediately, the Salvadorean "sandinistas" might be marching on the capital. And if the Nero-style solution mooted by President Romero was to be averted, the army had to step in yet again and save the nation and the military from themselves.

On October 15, they moved, and the coup brought a reforming junta into power. Unbalanced by the fall of Nicaragua, pressurised by the United States, and confronted by the domestic civil disorder and growing political violence, a progressive officer group found an appropriate moment to strike. Their success was largely due to the disarray among the traditional elites. In that moment of hesitation, they found the opportunity to launch a programme which promised much more than they had the strength to deliver. The coup of October 15 was carried out in political vacuum. It was an aberration which the oligarchy rapidly tried to rectify.

For a time there was the possibility of civil war as the various police forces, the national guard, the national police, and home police sat on the fence waiting to see what was going to happen. In Gotera, Morazan province, the commando unit was the last to declare loyalty to the new regime.

As General Romero ignominiously fled to Guatemala, the army issued a proclamation promising reforms demanded by the opposition in their Popular Platform. The young military officers also created a permanent committee, COPEFA—independent of the military authorities—to help monitor the agricultural reforms which were to concentrate mainly on the coffee, cotton and sugar cane industries. After a week of wheeling and dealing a Revolutionary Governmental Junta was formed.

The Junta was made up of two military men and three civilians, and it looked on the face of it to be a very hopeful and progressive political experiment. The coup had taken place with the support of Washington. The young military officers in COPEFA represented the reforming and professional trend in the Salvadorean army which first came to the fore in 1948 and again in 1961 for rather brief periods. They persuaded Dr Ramon Mayorga Quiroz, rector of the Simon Cañas Central American University to join the Junta along with the talented Guillermo Ungo, lawyer and leader of the social democratic party (MNR).

Moreover, to the satisfaction of COPEFA the progressive Colonel Adolfo Majano was elected—a man noted for his integrity. But there were problems filling the two remaining places with satisfactory people. The young officers wanted Colonel Rene Guerra y Guerra to take the other positon set aside for the army. That would have meant two reforming officers in the junta. But, according to some reports, the latter name was vetoed by Washington. The US proposed Colonel Jaime Gutierrez or Colonel Jose García.

COPEFA were faced with a dilemma. Failure to concede would result in the loss of support from Washington without which they could not hope either to survive politically or to carry out the ambitious programme of social reforms. Colonel Gutierrez joined the junta and Colonel García became minister of defence. The enforced choice of both men was to deal a serious blow to the credibility of the new junta and government. Despite the better judgement of COPEFA, the men were included and became immediately the Achilles heel of the political experiment.[45]

A further weakening of the Junta resulted from the selection of the engineer, Mario Antonio Andino, who represented private enterprise. From the very outset, COPEFA was forced to take on board at least three key people, García, Gutierrez and Andino—none of whom had anything in commom with the initiators of the October coup.

On October 23, the formation of a mainly civilian cabinet was announced. It included members of the Christian Democrat Party, the UDN and the MNR. Dr Ruben Ignacio Zamora, a Christian Democrat leader and the subject of an appeal by Amnesty International in April 1977, was appointed Ministero de la Presidencia, to link the cabinet with the junta.

In a statement announcing the coup, the colonels said that President Romero had come to power by means of a "scandalous election fraud" and that the country was in a state of "true economic and social disaster." Not surprisingly, with the junta using the rhetoric of reform, (and there is no reason to doubt the sincerity of the officers at that stage) Archbishop Romero recommended that the new regime should be given a chance to show its capabilities.

There were many close friends of Archbishop Romero both in the junta and in the cabinet. They joined more out of good faith than because of any deep confidence in the potential of the coup. Historical experience and political judgement almost dictated that sane public figures ought avoid such a high-risk venture. Yet the spirit of the October 15 coup provided the repressed opposition with a unique opportunity to confront the oligarchy under the constitution. The disarray on the right, due to the Nero-like ambitions entertained by the deposed General Romero, suddenly gave such talented

Social Democrats as Guillermo Ungo the chance to reform the "ungovernable" El Salvador.

Few men of good will could in conscience reject the call to office despite the obvious reservations about either the capability or the preparedness of the military high command to effect meaningful control over the security forces. On balance, Archbishop Romero and other leading clergy considered that the risk was worth taking. But the politicians all the time regarded the move as a leap in the dark. By late October, the mood was less sanguine in the capital.

Throughout, the campesinos remained sceptical. The Popular Organisations were less than charitable in their initial reaction to the junta and government. And they must bear some responsibility for the weakening of that experiment in representative government, even if the chances of success in that area were gloomy indeed. The Popular Organisations' reaction was rigidly ideological and stylised.

In fact the junta and its cabinet were rejected by BPR, FAPU and LP28, a federation of trade unions called FENESTRAS, and the guerrilla groups. The three main revolutionary groups argued that the coup and the promised reforms were nothing more than a US-inspired move to destroy the popular base and growing popularity of the opposition movements while maintaining the economic structure of the country intact for the continued enjoyment of the oligarchy or Fourteen Families. But that was not how the latter viewed the junta. The modest package of proposed reform was a little too much for the country's rich. The official party PCN, and other groups to the right such as ORDEN, UGB and FALANGE were less than enthusiastic about any talk of redistributing land. Archbishop Romero and Bishop Rivera Damas expressed the view that the church, while not allied to any party, welcomed genuine reform. The country's other four bishops were deeply suspicious of the junta's "communistic" tendencies.

The day of the coup, the LP28 and its guerrilla wing, ERP took over the working class suburbs and distributed arms, urging the people of the *turgurios* to rebel while they had the opportunity. The junta promptly declared a state of siege and for two days the military put down the incipient revolt with considerable bloodshed. The Red Cross were refused admission to tend to the wounded, some of whom literally bled to death. More violence followed. On October 22, police opened fire on the funeral of two murdered students and five of the mourners were killed. On October 23, the state of siege was lifted and two days later the Ministries of Labour and Economic Affairs were occupied without force by members of the BPR. Some 200, including three cabinet ministers, were held hostage. The occupation was criticised by Archbishop Romero as had been the attempted workers' revolt and its brutal repression.

On October 29, LP28 held a demonstration in San Salvador. The 300-strong unarmed parade got about two blocks before it was stopped outside the building of the pro-government *La Prensa Grafica*. Then marksmen opened up on the crowd from the roof, and the demonstrators scattered as a bomb exploded below just before the firing began. The strategy of this attack bears considerabale resemblance to what was to happen on March 30 during the funeral of Archbishop Romero. The LP28 found each street blocked off by a tank. A slaughter ensued. The remnant of the demonstration made its way to a church where they were forced to rip up the floor and bury 26 dead. They could get no guarantee from the police that the funeral of the victims would not be fired upon. The number killed in that particular protest has never been known for definite.[46]

On October 31, the BPR staged a parade satirising the junta. A lorry-load of police arrived and opened fire on the crowd.

Meanwhile, the junta was being presented with a list of demands from the popular movements, the guerrilla groups, the Church and the relatives of "disappeared" people. Two days after the coup, Archbishop Oscar Romero delivered a complete list of 176 people who had been captured and had disappeared under the previous regime and 15 political prisoners whose cases were still being tried. The International Red Cross sent a group to inspect the prisons and detention centres. But, at that stage, it seems that all the "secret cells" where torture was carried out had been destroyed and none of the "disappeared" people could be found.

However on November 6, the government set up a special commission to investigate the problem of the disappeared and the political prisoners. They were given sixty days to make a report which was to include a list of those responsible and compensation for the dependants of murdered people. The Commission began its work with a list of 199 political prisoners.

The junta outlined an ambitious reform programme: the old parliament was abolished, the supreme court was cleaned up and some 50 generals and colonels were dismissed from the armed forces and the police. Free elections were promised before 1982. On November 6, the government reached agreement with the BPR to secure the release of the hostages held in the ministries of Labour and Economic Affairs. In order to get the co-operation of the BPR, the authorities had agreed to disband ORDEN and not to increase the price of urban transport.

The following day, Dr Guillermo Ungo announced the dissolution of ORDEN because it had functioned as "a part of the repressive machinery and as an organ of domestic information of the repressive coups themselves." But according to Amnesty sources, although the staff and furniture of the ORDEN offices were removed from the Presidential Palace, little or nothing was done to dismantle the organisation in the countryside. That auxiliary force continued to assist the security forces. If anything demonstrated the impotence of the government, it was its failure to tackle the dismembering of the paramilitary organisation which had done so much to spread terror in the countryside.

When it is understood that the normal security force has only about 6,000 members, the most conservative estimates of ORDEN at 40,000 would indicate how crucial a role they have to play in implementing "repressive" policies.

The government was well-intentioned but it did not have the authority to carry out its programme.

But the goodwill created by the announcement of such a popular move provoked a positive response from the Popular Organisations. The BPR who had occupied the cathedral in San Salvador for two weeks left on November 11 while LP28 agreed to evacuate El Rosario Church. Plaza Libertad was evacuated by the Committee of Mothers of Political Prisoners. Land reform was the crucial question and the government did not disappoint, on paper at least. It was intended to collectivise land ownership in certain areas. The first stage planned to takeover farms of more than 500 hectares; and the following year it was hoped to extend the scheme to holdings between 150 and 500 hectares. There was a proposal to nationalise the banks and steps were taken to regulate the export of cotton, coffee and sugar. Maximum price orders were made for certain basic commodities and wages in the coffee and cotton sectors were increased.

In Washington, the State Department strongly encouraged support for the junta and provisions were made to send aid, while the US embassy in San Salvadore had a large team working very hard on the land reform programme. President Carter was said to favour very strongly the notion of bank nationalisation.

But the combination of street violence, the growing strength and audacity of the popular organisations, and the obvious determination of the such men in government as the Social Democrat Guillermo Ungo to initiate a programme of meaningful reform, provoked considerable disquiet in the ranks of the oligarchy. Such social and economic reforms would certainly result in political reform and the inevitable election of a popular government free from dependence on the military.

The reform programme also brought considerable strain within the military and oligarchic institutions. The close historical ties between wealth and military power ensured many colonels and generals success in the commercial world. In the past, any reform programme was very carefully scrutinised by the right and circumscribed by the conventions of mutual self-interest. Progressive reforms had been defeated in 1944 and 1960 by a political system which was very heavily weighted in favour of the oligarchy. The opposition could only exist at considerable cost to human life. And little seemed to have changed in the latter part of November.

Besides the attacks on demonstrations by the Popular Organisations, the right launched a massively expensive professional advertising campaign to promote the objectives of a movement entitled "Peace and Work". Wall-posters, newspaper advertisements and radio and television spots bombarded the public. Two major demonstrations were organised in San Salvador. The first saw upper and middle class women parade through the streets of the capital on December 10. Some sixty thousand took part in a highly organised march in San Salvador on December 27. In the three months, October, November and December, there were nearly one thousand deaths caused by political violence. The various right wing groups, Union Guerrera Blanca (UGB), the Organisation for Freedom from Communism, and the Anti-Communist Front for Central American Liberation (FALCO) were active. Moreover, the security forces in conjunction with ORDEN—disbanded in name only—were also directly involved in the killings.

Tension within the military and government was mounting towards the end of the year as the civilian members of the junta wanted their programme defined as anti-oligarchic. But COPEFA remained intranisgent on that point. Such a move would have brought the junta into direct conflict with the most powerful interests in the country.

At the beginning of December the special commission set up to investigate the whereabouts of political prisoners and the disappeared publicly recommended that the high officials who ordered the killings and so called "disappearances" should be brought to trial. They named as responsible the ousted General Romero and his immediate predecessor, Colonel Arturo Armando Molina. The head of national police Colonel Jose Antonio Lopez who had resigned,and the former directors of the national guard, General Alvaro Alvarenga and Jose Corleto were also named publicly by the commission. All are believed to be in Guatemala.

The commission's final report, made public on January 3, 1980, was a chilling reminder of what had been happening in El Salvador. Several clandestine cemeteries had been uncovered, one of which had thirty corpses. There were signs that many of the bodies had been brutally tortured and mutilated. The special commission found:

> In general terms, we can report that to date we have not found a single person of those who appear on the list of the disappeared; but on the other hand, we have proof of the capture of many of them by various official security forces, as in addition, at the present time there are no political prisoners or detainees in these places, according to reports of the directors, which we are delivering to the Minister of the Presidency of the Honourable Junta . . . all this brings us to the conclusion that we can presume that all the disappeared are dead.

The Commission had visited a prison and the General Directors' offices of the National Police, the National Guard and the Hacienda Police:

> In all these places we have found cells, dungeons and some cellars which could well have served as secret prisons or places where torture is carried out, although when we saw them, they were empty. We believe that these structures should be so modified as to make it impossible to use them as prisons.

The work of the commission was promptly shelved and gathered dust while the culprits, torturers and murderers, went free to repeat their acts of violence against the people of El Salvador.

47

Mass resignation followed the failure by the junta to meet a series of demands from the cabinet, issued on January 1, 1980, calling on it to exhibit proof of willingness to implement political and economic reforms; the cabinet also wanted to halt the swing to the right and take full control of the armed forces; and to expel the third member of the junta who, as a member of the business community, was held responsible for the swing to the right. When the ultimatum was not heeded, the two civilian members of the junta, Guillermo Ungo, leader of the National Revolutionary Movement (MNR) and Ramon Mayorga Quiroz quit followed by the entire civilian cabinet, many government officials and four fifths of the Supreme Court Judges. The Minister for Education, Salvador Samayoa, announced on January 8, that he was joining the Popular Liberation Forces (FLP).

At this point, the military felt completely isolated. And COPEFA cast around for new political partners. They held talks with the Christian Democrats (PDC) who agreed to join under certain conditions which appeared to have been met by the publication of a new programme on January 9 which promised to organise elections "as soon as possible", begin a dialogue with the left, and present new economic and social reforms. Among the new members of the junta were the President of the PDC, Jose Antonio Morales Erlich and Jose Napoleon Duarte, who joined on March 3, 1980.

The crisis within the new ruling junta and government forced the main popular organisations to unite with the title Coordinadora Nacional Revolucionaria de Masas. The BPR, the Ligas Populares and FAPU joined forces in a tactical alliance. A major demonstration was called for January 22—the forty eighth anniversary of the 1932 peasant massacre. But the days leading up to the protest were filled with tension. Rightwing elements, members of the Frente Amplio Nacional (FAN), took television time on the eighteenth, to denounce the "communist conspiracy" menacing El Salvador. Major Roberto D'Abuisson[47] who was a member of the security office during the regime of General Romero, outlined before the cameras the map of subversion in the country—naming names—and claimed that the communist party was the "head of the conspiracy". The Union Guerrera Blanca (UGB) announced publicly that it would halt the spread of communism in spite of the apparent inefficiency of the armed forces.

A number of prominent public figures, including some named by D'Abuisson, were murdered. And workers and activists assembled at the university in preparation for the demonstration were bombed and machine-gunned. Nevertheless between 80,000 and 150,000 turned up in the capital for the protest march despite the inevitability of violence. The march was much larger than those organised by the "Crusade for Peace and Work" the previous month. The huge file of workers, *campesinos,* students and inhabitants of the *tugurios* walked in an orderly fashion through the streets. But, as the FAPU section passed by the Palacio Nacional and into the square in front of the cathedral, gunmen opened fire on the marchers from the windows above. The shooting began from the Palacio Nacional about 1.00; and the demonstrators took refuge in the cathedral and in the church of El Rosario. The latter group, which included quite a number of journalists, were attacked by the National Police, whose barracks was only two blocks away. About 3.00 o'clock the centre of the city was surrounded by tanks. About twenty-one had died in the violence and one hundred and twenty were wounded.

Throughout the day the government controlled radio and television was quiet except for a few perfunctory communiques. At 7.45 p.m. the junta regretted the tragic events of the day. According to the statement, the protest took place in a climate of order and tranquility until persons unknown opened fire on the demonstration. The junta insisted that the armed forces had been kept in barracks in order to prevent provocation.

In early April, 1980 the Democratic Salvadorean Front (FSD) was established, and it included Guillermo

Ungo's Social Democratic National Revolutionary Movement (MNR) and a section of the PDC which included two important ministers from the first government after the coup, and many others who had been closely associated with the reforming junta of October 15, 1979. Later in April, the FSD joined with the left to found the Democratic Revolutionary Front (FDR) with the former Minister, Alvarez Cordova, as secretary-general. The committee had representatives from BPR, FAPU, LP28, MNR, and the communist National Democratic Union (UDN).

Such an unlikely coalition could only have been held together by the combined opposition to repression and flagrant transgression of human rights in a country where the radical right had shut the door firmly on political change through constitutional means.

The result of this political alliance is that one can no longer speak of a political centre grouping in Salvador. There remains the junta and the government recruited from the Christian Democratic Party and the military. But they appear to be either powerless or unwilling to halt the violence.

Effective control of the country lies with the parallel government—that shadowy group of military, oligarchy, and para-military rightwing forces who govern by mandate of terror.

The popular mandate now lies with the FDR. They now have diplomatic representatives in many capitals. In a democratic El Salvador the future would lie with the Front which has attracted some of the most talented and most respected public figures in the country. But, if it has taken patience and dedication to build up such an organisation with an obvious wealth of talent at national level, considerable insight into the ideology of national security can also be gained by focussing on the harsh realities at local level.

THE REVOLT OF FREDY ANTONIO VASQUEZ[48]

In an effort to understand the process of radicalisation in El Salvador during the past few years, it is possible to study the growth in political consciousness of one man who has become a victim of the random violence and repression so prevalent in his country during 1980.

Antonio Vasquez was born in Pedemal, Chilanga in the Department of Morazan. Becoming a catechist, he found considerable satisfaction in his work. From the outset he harboured an instinctive dislike for the unjust social system in Salvador. For example, when he and other young catechists prepared a lesson on the seventh commandment, he highlighted the community aspects of stealing: To hoard at a time of grain scarcity, he wrote, was stealing, as was also the practice of selling at inflated prices when the peasant had no alternative but to buy or starve. He argued that the inequitable distri-

bution of land was stealing, as also was the existence of an all-powerful oligarchy.

Tonio had shown considerable interest and enthusiasm for attempting to reform society by democratic means. In 1976, the so called *transformación agraria* was launched by Colonel Arturo Molina. Less than 5% of the country's land was to be affected. Thousands of new peasant proprietors were to be created. The deal was sold to the oligarchy as an investment against revolution. It was supported by the US. But only a small section of the fourteen families were converted to the scheme. The de Sola family one of the largest and wealthiest of the oligarchy, favoured the move. But they could make very few converts among the other thirteen families. Molina was attacked in the rightwing press as a "communist" and a socialist. Nothing could have been further from the truth. But judging by the reaction to such a modest proposal, the "not an inch" mentality of the oligarchy reacted vigorously to even the slightest suggestion of moderate reform. The *transformación agraria* was abandoned.

From Tonio's standpoint the defeat of the agrarian reform plan did not signify the end of his confidence in the constitutional path. He threw himself into the presidential election campaign of 1977, more in desperation than in the hope of achieving anything substantial. He still clung to the legal path, and, despite the widespread boycott of the contest by most political parties, he supported and worked very hard for the opposition candidate. The PCN candidate, General Carlos Humberto Romero, won by default; and his victory was made absolutely certain by massive electoral fraud. Tonio had been working in some of the polling stations and had seen people coming in armed and throwing out those who voted for the opposition party. He saw voting papers being piled into the ballot boxes already marked for Romero. He had seen so much that day that, according to one source, he was so sickened that he went to a friend and said there was no alternative but to join a popular organisation.

He joined the LP28 and the Ligas Populares. He felt constrained by his work as a catechist. The blanket denial of human rights gave a spur to this obvious idealism. It is clear that he rose rapidly in the ranks of popular organisation and soon found himself in the capital, planning and working out national strategies. But his real strength was working in his home area. Although very young, he was one of the most important opposition leaders in the country.

Very reliable sources testify that his movement to fulltime politics did not presage a rejection of Catholicism: his commitment to the radical teaching of the Gospel remained his inspiration. So much so that he remained a source of inspiration and admiration for a number of clergy and religious who knew him very well. He was a difficult man to keep track of as his work kept him constantly on the move. He was on the death list, and he knew that capture by the *guardia* meant summary execution, if he was lucky. A slow death after torture was a more likely and typical end for a man of his importance. The more influential he became within the *ligas,* the more wanted he was by the police.

Moreover, Antonio was not impressed by the reforming potential of the October 15, 1979, coup. On the 29th of that month he went up to the capital with a group of *ligas* supporters to demonstrate in the climate of newfound freedom. But when about 300 demonstrators were passing the *Prensa Grafica* building, snipers opened fire from the roof as a bomb exploded in the street below. As the group tried to disperse through side-streets they found their way cut off by the military using trucks and tanks. At least seventy died that day, according to the organisers. A remnant retreated back to a church in the centre carrying the bodies of over twenty comrades.

They were forced to bury them under the floor of the building when they failed to win assurances from the police that a funeral procession would not be fired upon. The incident cured Antonio of any illusions about the reforming intentions of the junta. Within a matter of two weeks, the conciliatory spirit of the coup was evaporating.

On January 14, he was taken from a bus by the national guard at the turn-off for Delicias de Concepción. They found that he was carrying paints and spray cans—the type used for writing on walls. The *guardia* were seen to kick him on the head. He was then taken to Osicala. The next morning, he was found dead in the jail of the mayor's office with a note tied on him, saying traitors beware, etc.[49] It is clear that the *guardia* were attempting to make the killing look like the work of the popular organisations.

It was subsequently learned that the *guardia* from Osicala had been informed about Tonio by the *commandante* from his home-town of Pedemal. And after the *guardia* had finished "interrogating" their captive, they made the *commandante* travel to Osicala to administer the *coup de grâce*. He did so reluctantly and it is believed that the fatal shot was fired by the informant. Some months later the *commandante* was shot dead.

Antonio was one of many hundreds of *campesinos* who have died in such a manner. His body showed signs of torture—all his fingers were broken—but that is not unusual in a country where violence to prisoners is a matter of course.

The repression against catechists continued to get much more severe in the early months of 1980 as an extract from this letter written by a young Christian suggests: The writer was afraid to go to Mass in the cantone because they had learned that they were "on the list". Other catechists had received similar threats against their lives. But the person wrote with great courage:

I am prepared for whatever happens. But it makes me a little sad because I love my community very much and we have done so little. However, if God has so disposed, well then I accept it and he surely knows why.[50]

Chapter Two

THE MAKING OF A MARTYR

Christ, Christ Jesus,
identify with us,
Lord, Lord, my God,
identify with us.
Christ, Christ Jesus,
throw in your lot
not with the oppressor class
that squeezes and devours the community,
but with the oppressed,
with my people who are thirsty for peace.

Misa campesina

Only two days after fraudulent elections had placed General Carlos Romero in power, Oscar Arnulfo Romero (no relation) was named Archbishop of San Salvador on February 22, 1977. His appointment was not greeted with wild enthusiasm by those who championed the cause of human rights within the church. He was seen to be very much the moderate tending towards conservatism on doctrinal questions and most traditional in his attitude towards authority. The fact that Romero was chosen at all reflected the serious divisions within the Salvadorean Church. But if the progressive forces had not secured the selection of the Bishop of Santiago de Maria, Monseñor Rivera Damas, for the post, they at least had blocked successfully the appointment of the ultra-conservative Colonel José Eduardo Alvares, Bishop of San Miguel. At one point, there had been complete deadlock and Romero emerged as a "safe" compromise.

Up to the point of taking over in the capital, Monseñor Romero's life had been distinguished by hard work and dedication to the priestly ministry. In no sense had he emerged as a natural leader of the Salvadorean Church. His road to martyrdom had begun in the inauspicious way of most of his fellow countrymen. Born in the remote town of Ciudad Barrios, on August 15, 1917, he experienced the grinding poverty of the campo. His parents, Santos Romero and Guadalupe de Jesus Galdámez, were never well off. They worked for the telecommunications company, ANTEL, and the young Oscar used to make some money for the family by delivering telegrams.

Oscar Romero first went to the minor seminary run by the Claretians then on to the major seminary in San Miguel and later to the national seminary in the capital which was run by the Jesuits. He remained there until 1937 before moving to Rome where he studied at the Gregorian University until 1943, and was awarded a licentiate in theology. He had been ordained in Rome a year earlier. But his time in Italy, particularly during the war, was one of isolation from his home and friends and extreme poverty. There too he experienced at first hand the authoritarianism of facism and the suffering it brought in its wake.

When he returned to Salvador he was sent to work in his own area where he quickly established a reputation for himself as a very conscientious priest dedicated to his pastoral duties. Above all, he is remembered in the region as having time for everybody, rich and poor alike. His door was always open to provide advice, consolation or just to hear of the sufferings of the downtrodden—a story he knew from personal experience.

But if Romero was popular there, among the rich and poor alike, he also had the reputation of being a very strict taskmaster with his priests. He had been named titular bishop of Tambee in 1967. Three years later he was nominated auxiliary bishop of San Salvador and in 1974 he became bishop of the remote diocese of Santiago de Maria—a position he held until his recall to the capital as archbishop three years later.

In order to understand Romero's stern attitude towards his clergy it is necessary to recall quickly the history of the Catholic Church in that country. About 81% of the total population is Catholic, while the country is an ecclesiastical province composed of an arch-diocese and four dioceses. After the establishment of San Salvador diocese in 1842, no others were organised until 1913 when Santa Ana and San Miguel were set up. Santiago de Maria diocese was created in 1954, and San Vicente in 1958. The diocese of San Salvador was raised to an archdiocese in 1929.

Every effort had been made to increase the number of priests and parishes to keep pace with the expanding population. In 1944, there were 106 parishes, with 203 priests and 357 nuns. By 1970, the number of parishes had increased to 175 with 372 priests and 803 nuns. There was a serious pastoral problem created by the fact that over 200 of the priests in 1970 belonged to religious orders, mainly Salesians and Jesuits. Only about 50% of the religious were involved in parish work; 20% were tied to teaching while a further 10% were working in seminaries, and the remainder in the work of the archdiocese. In Salvador the Catholic Church had 117 schools with 31,000 students.[1]

Traditionally, with so many priests involved in insti-tutions, there was considerable neglect of the pastoral duties of the Church in the countryside. In 1970, the archdiocese of San Salvador had fewer than 20,000 inhabitants per priest while the diocese of San Miguel had over 30,000. The latter diocese was even in a much worse pastoral position than the figures might indicate; the remoteness of parishes in the countryside required constant travel by dedicated priests who could be called upon to work up to 20 hours a day. The situation today is not very much better although there is much greater emphasis on pastoral work.

What made Romero not a little unpopular among some sectors of the clergy was his determination to demand of them the same dedicated hard work he demanded of himself. The Salvadorean church has had many serious problems, and not the least of these has been the lack of idealism among a small sector of the clergy who sought an easy life. That was not how Romero viewed the priestly ministry.

Many of the younger clergy had not remained unaffected by the pace of political change in Salvador. They presented a radical critique of society, and demanded rapid social reform. The more leftwing of these clergy did not welcome the appointment of the new archbishop with great enthusiasm. Yet he had a reputation for speaking his mind no matter what the consequences might be. He was fearless and frank and preached with ,a conviction which was very moving. His oratorical powers had made him a popular choice at every fiesta. Yet in San Salvador that aspect of his character was not as appreciated as it was in the campo. In the capital, he was still a middle-of-the-roader.

Rutilio Grande: champion of the poor

Yet it took only one tragic event to evoke the real character and leadership qualities of that shy, diffident man. One week after becoming Archbishop, his close friend and leading Jesuit intellectual, Rutilio Grande, was murdered along with a 72-year-old man and a boy of 16 when their jeep was machine-gunned in Aguilares on March 12, 1977.[2]

Rutilio Grande was educated in Spain and was for a time president of the national seminary in the capital before it was closed by the bishops. He had worked as a parish priest in Aguilares. He had contributed a tremendous amount of work to changing the pastoral orientation of the local church towards a more radical Christian perspective, trying to have the teachings of the Second Vatican Council and Medellin given practical outlet in Salvador where the majority of the bishops were less than enthusiastic to embark on any "theology of crisis".

But the bond between Romero and Rutilio Grande was more than friendship. Both men shared a common vision of society, although the Jesuit was a little more advanced in his thinking than the future archbishop.

Rutilio Grande was partially responsible for changing the entire Jesuit philosophy in central America with his "primary and fundamental option" which envisaged "a pastoral team working in either rural area or in a slum to promote Christian conscientisation". He chose Aguilares, a remote area in sugar cane and cotton country where about 70% of the people lived in poverty. But why was he murdered?

A banner carried by a small girl in the town of Apopa read: "Jesus Christ is with us when we denounce injustice". In simple form, Rutilio Grande was the victim of institutionalised violence and social injustice—the first clerical casualty in a country where so many ordinary people had died because of their struggle for dignity. On February 13, 1977, he had preached a sermon to mark the expulsion of a priest friend from the country, using the following prophetic words: "It was a matter of being or not being faithful to the mission of Jesus here and now. And for being faithful there would be reprisals, calumnies, blows, torture, kidnappings, bombs and, if one was an outsider, expulsion. But there always remained the fundamental question: it is dangerous to be a Christian in our milieu! It is practically illegal to be an authentic Christian in our environment . . . precisely because the world which surrounds us is founded radically on an established disorder before which the mere proclamation of the Gospel is subversive".

He went on to say that he heard that soon the Bible and the Gospel would not be allowed to pass the Salvadorean frontiers. Only the covers would get through because all the pages were "subversive, against sin, of course". And if Jesus Christ were to return as before travelling from Galilee to Judea, "that is to say from Chalatenango to San Salvador, I fear that he would not arrive; because of his actions and words at Apopa, he would be detained and imprisoned at Guazapa".[3]

Rutilio Grande added that Jesus would probably be crucified, accused of being factious, with strange and exotic ideas contrary to Democracy, "that is, against the minority". Some preferred a dumb Christ, without a mouth, passing on a portable platform through the streets. A Christ with a muzzle, a Christ made according to our whim and our petty interests. Some did not want a questioning God who disturbed our consciences. A God who would ask: Cain, what have you done to your brother Abel? Some would prefer a God in the clouds. They do not want that Jesus of Nazareth for "in Christianity one has to be ready to give one's life in the service of securing a just order, in saving the majority and in helping defend the values of the Gospel."[4]

Rutilio Grande paid the ultimate price for his commitment. An article in *Orientación* described the murder of the Jesuit as an attack on the Church and an attack on all those who desired liberation for the people "and when we say liberation, we say it in the sense of breaking the bonds of sin which prevent the realisation of peace, justice and love in society. And the products of that sin are: poverty and hunger, undernourished children, broken families, abandoned children, unemployment, violence and deception of the people."[5]

The murder of Rutilio Grande had a profound effect on Archbishop Romero. He is reported to have spent hours praying beside the body. It was his moment of truth.

The new archbishop acted swiftly; he demanded an explanation from the authorities, excommunicated those responsible and refused to take part in any official ceremony until the killing was solved and the murderers brought to justice. This led him to boycott the presidential inauguration of Gen. Carlos Romero on July 1, 1977.

He set up a permanent committee to monitor human rights in the country, closed the Catholic schools and colleges for three days, and cancelled all religious services on Sunday, March 20, except for a single Mass in front of the cathedral attended by an estimated 100,000 people. Ironically, the next time a similar crowd was to gather in the Plaza Barrios outside the cathedral was on March 30, 1980, for the funeral service of the murdered archbishop himself.

An editorial in the archdiocesan magazine *Orientación* of March 27 posed a serious question about divisions within the Church of El Salvador:

> We ask ourselves. Will there be two churches in El Salvador? Those who feel the assassination of a priest and those who don't. Those who suffer with their tortured brothers and the unjustly persecuted, and those who will not. Those who think and feel with the Pope and the bishops and those who think, they have the deposit of the true Faith.[6]

There were many who believed that they held "the deposit of the true faith". On the right, a combination of self-interest, greed and a widespread belief in a world communist conspiracy propelled groups to greater and more brutal violence. There were certainly very serious social divisions within the church. And the members of ORDEN, many of whom viewed themselves as being exemplary catholics, did not take kindly to the *"betrayal"* of men like Rutilio Grande. The Church had begun to meddle in matters which did not concern it, according to the military and the right.

Conflict in a changing church

But the most serious challenge facing Archbishop Romero immediately after coming to the capital was the need to heal the divisions within the national hierarchy. The conference of El Salvadorean bishops was a constant source of disappointment to Monseñor Romero. It consisted of five bishops and the auxiliary of San Salvador. Up until the time of his death, the archbishop fought manfully to bring about some form of unity, but he met with little or no success.

Romero could only rely upon the support of Rivera Damas, the bishop of Santiago and former auxiliary in the archdiocese. His main opponents were the Bishop of San Vicente, Pedro Arnoldo Aparicio y Quintanilla, who was also president of the episcopal conference; and José Eduardo Alvarez, chaplain in chief to the armed forces' the bishop of San Miguel.[7]

It is not too far-fetched to suggest that the rift in the Salvadorean church was echoed in the sixteenth century, the age of discovery. Both Spain and Portugal were badly divided on what attitude to take to the Indians. There was a humanistic school of thought and the royalist or realist camp. The former, who numbered the Dominicans and the Jesuits in their ranks, argued that the indigenous populations were citizens of the kingdom of God entitled to the rights of any Portuguese or Spaniard. Consequently, they could not have their lands seized, be press-ganged into forced labour camps and mines or endure violent conversion to Christianity.

The royalist school, conversely, regarded the Indians from an aristocratic height as being inferior creatures. There was some doubt for a while as to whether they might have souls. Not surprisingly, such base opinions of the Indians provided the conquerors with quite considerable scope. Legal theories based on such views offered little solace to the indigenous populations. The Amerindians were the victims of repression and brutality.

The Church had a very mixed role in the process of conquest. There were the "defenders of the Indians" as some bishops were called with justification. But there were also those who sought the advantages of conversion with the aid of the sword rather than exclusively by use of the Cross and the Word of God.

Despite the gap of centuries there are many similarities between the opposing philosophies in the age of conquest and today. Some members of the Church seek through co-existence with the national security state to secure progress and protection for the faithful by diplomacy and tact—by being close to the centre of power. But others have taken an opposite view, the preferential option for the poor; and that philosophical position has led them into considerable difficulty with the civil authorities. Archbishop Romero found himself in deep conflict with the Salvadorean authorities over his bias for the destitute, the exploited and the deprived.

He was very much in the tradition of Bartolomé de las Casas and fellow Dominican, Antonio de Montesinos, *los protectores de los indios*. On the Sunday before Christmas of 1511, the latter preached to a congregation of colonists in Hispaniola (Santo Domingo) on the rights of the Indians. He shocked his complacent listeners to the bone. His words were to reverberate through Latin American history and be taken up again in the twentieth century by men like Romero. On that Sunday in 1511, nearly five hundred years ago, Montesinos said:

In order to make your sins against the Indians known to you I have come up in this pulpit, I who am a voice of Christ crying in the wilderness of this island, and therefore it behoves you to listen, not with careless attention, but with all your heart and senses, so that you may hear it; for this is going to be the strangest voice that you ever heard, the harshest and hardest and most awful and most dangerous that ever you expected to hear . . . this voice says that you are in mortal sin, that you live and die in it, for the cruelty and tyranny you use in dealing with these innocent people. Tell me by what right or justice do you keep these Indians in such a cruel and horrible servitude? On what authority have you waged a detestable war against these people, who dwell quietly and peacefully in their own lands? Why do you keep them so oppressed and weary, not giving them enough to eat nor taking care of them in their illness? For with the excessive work you demand of them they fall ill and die, or rather you kill them with your desire to extract and acquire gold every day. And what care do you take that they should be instructed in religion? Are these not men? Have they not rational souls? Are you not bound to love them as you love yourselves? Be certain that, in such a state as this, you can no more be saved than the Moors or Turks.[8]

But the other Dominican mentioned, Bartolomé de las Casas (1474-1566) has become much more widely known than his fiery confrère. His life was marked by public controversy, and for his time he wrote a series of "best sellers" the most popular being *Brevísima relación de la destrucciónió de las indias*, a strong indictment of the colonists. He worked hard to expose the violence against the Indians; and in 1542 the New Laws were proclaimed by the king of Spain which reorganised the council of the Indies, prohibited Indian slavery, and sought the gradual suppression of the *encomienda* system, whereby "the Indians of conquered regions were parcelled out by royal grant to individual Spaniards, and compelled to render them forced labour in their fields and in the mines."

An indication of just how basic the debate became following colonisation, is reflected in the Bull *Sublimis Deus* of Paul III which declared officially that Indians had souls, that they were rational creatures, capable of self government and also capable of freely embracing Christianity. But despite the titanic struggle by de las Casas and many others to defend the rights of the Indians, the indigenous populations continued to be treated very harshly by their "masters". The feelings which gave rise to the *Leyenda negra* have all too unfortunately a very solid historical foundation.

De las Casas returned to Central America in 1544, as the Bishop of Chiapa; but he was not very successful in imposing the New Laws even in his own diocese. Yet despite the many failures, he was succeeded by many other clerics who defended the poor with considerable courage.

However, besides the humanist tradition among the Latin American hierarchy, there was also the rival and more dominant royalist school of thought. The latter

64

made their peace with the secular powers and preached divine resignation in the face of suffering, social injustice and deprivation. In the twentieth century, external domination has given way to "internal colonialism", and while there is no debate over whether the Indians have souls there is considerable evangelical concern over the rights of the poor which are not respected by the national security state. In Salvador, Romero was very much in the "humanist tradition" of de las Casas. But he was out-numbered by "royalist" bishops.

There has been a tendency in many contemporary studies of the Latin American Church to divide the clergy rather crudely into such general categories as conservative and progressive, liberal and reactionary. Such conceptualisation often does violence to the facts. Reality is seldom quite so simple. Thus it is possible to have a conservative bishop in a more traditional theological sense who might prove to be a staunch and outspoken defender of human rights in a repressive regime. In another instance, a man of advanced views relating to moral theology might prove quite a disappointment in the campaign to defend the poor and the wretched.

But when the spotlight is turned on Salvador, the situation virtually deteriorates into caricature. Archbishop Romero was opposed in his every action by rivals within the national episcopal conference. Moreover, he was the subject of a malicious campaign of calumny. Yet Romero did not retaliate in kind. He retained his composure and a deep respect for his fellow bishops, men who differed from him radically in their conception of the Christian mission.

Rival pastorals

The divisions within the hierarchy were a matter of public knowledge and a Christian scandal. On one occasion, the rival groups produced counter pastorals giving contradictory advice in certain instances. Where Romero and Rivera Damas were scholarly and unemotional, their rivals were polemical, patronising and inept. Romero and Rivera Damas, in *The Church, political organisations and violence,*[9] brought out on August 6, 1978, outlined a defence of the right to organise among the peasants, a right that was defended by the United Nations' Declaration of Human Rights, and by *Pacem in Terris* and *Gaudium et Spes*.

According to the pastoral, organisations which supported the government had "complete freedom" while those that voiced opposition found themselves impeded or prevented from exercising their right to organise legally and work for their aims, "just though these may be." That discrimination resulted in the fact that the "economically powerful minorities can organise in defence of their interests and very often to the detriment of the great majority of the people." The pastoral added that no one could take away, least of all from the poor, the right to organise, because the protection of the weak "is the principal purpose of laws and of social organisations." But in defending the right of association the two bishops were not defending "terrorist groups or supporting anarchist movements and irrationally subversive ideologies." They had in the past "often denounced any cult of violence or class hatred," and they had "reiterated the principle of our Christian moral teaching that the end does not justify criminal means and that there is no freedom to do evil."

The pastoral denounced the dangerous and evil minded oversimplification which sought to misrepresent demands as terrorism and unlawful subversion. But the pastoral was quite concerned to point out that the Church has a purely religious function, that it was there to serve the people and finally it has a role in the struggle for liberation in Christian salvation. Romero and Rivera Damas were quite clear on the distinction between faith and politics, and they warned those who had a political vocation "to profess their faith openly so that it becomes their ultimate point of reference and they can grow in it. Yet, in their theoretical convictions and in detailed applications, they must not fall into the temptation of pride and intransigence as though the legitimate political choice to which their faith has led them were the only way of working wholeheartedly for justice."

Perhaps the most important part of the pastoral dealt with the judgement of the Church on violence. The "most acute form in which violence appears on our continent and in our country is what the bishops of Medellin called "institutionalised violence," where "the majority of men and women and above all the children in our country find themselves deprived of the necessities of life;" that violence found its expression in the structure and daily functioning of a socio-economic and political system which accepts it as normal and usual that progress is impossible unless the majority of the people are used as a productive force under the management of a privileged minority. Those responsible for "this institutionalisation of violence, as they are responsible for the international structures which cause it, are those who monopolise economic power instead of sharing it." Such violence was "firmly and dramatically established in" Salvador, according to the pastoral.

In turn, that gives rise to "repressive violence" where the minority try to "contain the aspirations of the majority, violently crushing any signs of protest against the injustices we have mentioned." But the pastoral then goes on to outline its attitude to various forms of violence and when it is legitimate for the Christian to defend himself with arms. And it concludes with an appeal:

To all our Catholics, to our brothers and sisters of other Churches, and to all men of good will, reminding them that the Lord is present and that His voice speaks to us also from the misery of our people. Let us hear Him: "What you do to the least of my brethren you do to me" *(Matthew* 25:40).

To those who possess economic power, the Lord of the world says that they should not close their eyes selfishly to this situation. They should understand that only by sharing in justice and brotherhood with those

67

who do not have this power can they cooperate for the good of the country, and will they enjoy that peace and happiness which cannot come from wealth accumulated at the expense of others. Listen to Him.

To the middle class, who have already assured a minimum of dignity for their lives, Jesus points out that there remains a majority who still do not have enough to live on. He urges them to support the poor and the peasants and not to be content with making their own gains secure. Listen to Him.

To the professional associations and to the intellectuals, the Divine Master, who is the light of all understanding, says that they should use their scientific and technical expertise to investigate the problems of our country and fulfil their professional obligations by looking for solutions to them. They should publicly declare their interest in the welfare of the country and not take refuge in an uncommitted knowledge and science, in a calm seclusion remote from the suffering of people. Hear Him.

Of the political parties and "popular organisations" which have been the main concern of this pastoral letter, Christ, the guide of nations and of history, requires that they learn to put their concern for the poor majority before their own interests, that they use the political system effectively and with justice and press honourably and boldly for the beginning of the transformation for which we long. Obey Him.

To the public authorities, who have the sacred duty of governing for the good of all, Christ, the Kings of Kings and Lord of Lords, addresses a call for a sense of truth, justice and of sincere service to the people.

Therefore:
1. let them pass laws which take into account the majority of people who live in the countryside

where there are serious problems about land, wages and medical, social and educational facilities;

2. let them genuinely widen the narrow area of political discussion and give formal and real admission to the various political voices in the country;

3. let them give an opportunity to organise legally to those who have been unjustly deprived of this human right, especially the peasants;

4. let them take notice of the people's rejection of the Law for the Defence and Maintenance of Public Order and in its place let them promulgate other laws which do in fact guarantee human rights and peace; let them establish adequate channels for civil and political dialogue, so that no-one need be afraid to express ideas which may benefit the common good, even if they imply a criticism of the government;

5. let them stop the terrorisation of the peasantry and put an end to this tragic situation of confrontation between peasants, exploiting their poverty to organise some under the projection of the government and persecuting others just because they have organised themselves independently of the government to seek a reasonable standard of living and their rights;

6. let them win the confidence of the people with some intelligent and generous gestures such as the following: an amnesty for all prisoners who have not yet been brought before any court but who have "disappeared" after being captured by the security forces; and a chance of returning home to all those who have been expelled or who are unable to return to El Salvador for political reasons.

We believe that all this is the will of the Divine Saviour of the world and that the Father's command is: *He must be listened to!*

The other Salvadorean bishops saw the situation regarding the organisations somewhat differently. In the counter-pastoral,[10] issued on August 28, 1978, they admitted "that one cannot deny anyone the right to association for honest and just ends without breaking the natural law." But they went on to point out that those who followed a Marxist line were not Christian; while for their part, the Marxists insinuated that they were the most genuine and authentic expression of Christianity. And they warned priests, religious and lay people of the danger of "falling into the temptation of reducing the mission of the Church to the merely temporal aspect; the objectives of the gospel to an anthropocentric perspective, salvation to material well-being and the creativity of the Church to a political compromise.

They concluded that leftist political organisations such as FECCAS the Christian Federation of Campesinos of Salvador and the Union of Rural Workers (UTC), "are not organised by the Church, and it therefore follows that they do not have the right to claim for themselves the protection of the Church or instrumentalise it for their own ends." Priests were warned not to co-operate with those organisations that were strictly in the temporal plane and were, what was more, organisations of the Left.

The fundamental conflict within the hierarchy could not have been greater on the question of the popular organisations. They were worlds apart. It was almost as if the two rival groups were speaking about entirely different countries, so different were their perspectives on the opposition groups. It would be quite fair to say that FECCAS enjoyed the support of many clergy. Indeed, support meant active involvement for some and a life "on the run" as priests moved clandestinely around the countryside.

Both Romero and Rivera Damas were careful to maintain a distance, a principle some of the clergy were imprudent enough not to observe. Overt political commitment provoked considerable tension between Monseñor Romero and some of his more active priests and seminarians. That rigorous stance, transcending partisan political commitment, was the archbishop's greatest defence and strength. He could be accused of many things but the charges could never be substantiated. Romero was on the side of the poor. He was their champion, the voice of the voiceless, the brutalised and the "disenfranchised."

His many conservative rivals, both clerical and lay, feared most the creation of a Church with a strong and caring social conscience which would preach, without fear or self-interest, the radical message of the Gospel and the teachings of the papacy as reflected in the recent encyclicals of John XXIII, Paul VI and John Paul II. "If a brother or a sister be naked," says Saint James "if they lack their daily nourishment, and one of you says to them: 'Go in peace, be warmed and be filled,' without giving them what is necessary for the body, what good does it do?"[11] Building on that principle, Paul VI taught in *On the Development of Peoples:* "If certain landed estates impede the general prosperity because they are extensive, unused or poorly used, or because they bring hardship to people or are detrimental to the interests of the country, the common good sometimes demands their expropriation."[12] In his rather unique style, Archbishop Romero translated Church social teaching into the language demanded by the needs of the Latin American Church. He was helped on that course by the documents of Medellin and the writings of liberation theologians.

The pastoral message of the Church in Latin America has been forged in the harsh, repressive experience of a sub-continent where respect for human rights from government is the exception rather than the general rule. There is a sense of primitive Christianity where religion has been shorn of all accretions and exposed in

71

all its stark simplicity as gospel of love. Much of that achievement must reflect on the work of the *Consejo Episcopal Latinoamericano* (CELAM) which was founded in June, 1958 and is centred in Bogotá, Colombia.

Latin American bishops had met for the first time at Rio de Janeiro, Brazil, in 1955; and CELAM was born three years later. But it was the episcopal conference at Medellin, Colombia, in 1968 which proved to be the watershed for the local church. Encouraged by the radical encyclical *On the Development of Peoples*, the bishops listened to men like Helder Camara of Recife who spoke of "the main fruits — rotten fruits — of capitalist egoism" where "internal colonialism" was spreading, allowing "a small group of privileged people in Latin America itself whose wealth is maintained at the expense of the poverty of millions of their fellow-citizens." Dom Helder spoke of owners who held large tracts of land kept deliberately uncultivated where poor families were allowed to live without any hope or right to holdings: "care is taken that they are kept in foul hovels and work under a patriarchal regime without any law to support them. This is unquestionably a sub-human situation, white slavery."[13]

Jon Sobrino, summed up the message of Medellin as the concrete Latin American implementation of Vatican II. The documents created an impact because of their actual content and not because they were authoritative episcopal texts: "the message of Medellin was already in seedling form, certainly in hope; the reality of the continent."[14]

The words of Helder Camara on the rotten fruits of capitalist egoism were echoed in the final documents which had a particularly down-to-earth tone. They expressed a "partisan alliance with the poor." But the Church not only "lent its voice to the poor but sought out their voice and let it sound out within the churches. It decentralised and gave up its wordly character by establishing solidarity with the poor. In many ecclesial groups it succeeded in establishing an unfamiliar degree of unity between bishops, priests, religious men and women, and the laity. It set up new ministries, not just to fill a gap but to find new and rich resources in pastoral agents, peasants, labourers, and indigenous peoples. It bravely faced up to persecution and martyrdom, seeing all of them as privileged signs of its truth. The Church produced new forms of theological reflection, from grassroots thoughts to the fully articulated ideas of theologians. All of them were designed to be of service, both within the Church and in its mission."[15] That struggle for liberation in the world brought its own internal liberation which freed the Church to face the real issues of the day.

For Monseñor Romero, as it was for many other like-minded prelates, the consequences of such a commitment were profound. "My job seems to be to go around picking up insults and corpses," he once remarked when the church of Aguilares, where Rutilio Grande ministered, was returned to him.[16] The Jesuits were held in the highest suspicion by some of the Salvadorean bishops who felt that Romero had become completely mesmerised by that order.[17] In the small Jesuit house, in the suburbs of San Salvador, one room has about twenty bullet marks where the house was sprayed with machinegun fire late one night by a right-wing group. Fortunately on that occasion nobody was wounded. Since then the house was destroyed by two explosions. Others have not been so lucky.[18]

The Church which Monseñor Romero inherited as Archbishop of San Salvador was one which had reflected very seriously on the documents of Medellin; and his predecessor in the capital, Dr Luis Chavez y Gonzalez, must take considerable credit for actively encouraging his priests to put the new social Christianity into practice. The Salvadorean Church did not suddenly lurch towards "radicalism" under Romero, provoking serious divisions within the hierarchy and clergy. For many years, the local Church was highly conservative. Many of the hierarchy were profoundly out of touch with and radically opposed to social innovations in Catholic

73

teaching. But Archbishop Chavez broke ranks with his conservative colleagues after Medellín and responded to the new insights of the Latin American Church.

Archbishop Chavez had said in a pastoral letter in August 1975 that the best land was dedicated to coffee, cotton and sugar-cane for export, while only the worst land remained to provide Salvadoreans with their daily bread. He also maintained that 92% of pre-school children suffered from malnutrition and that only 35% of the men were employed throughout the whole year. The Archbishop also encouraged the setting up of base communities[19] — small Christian groups designed to provide community structures for people where the notion of a conventional parish was quite unsuited.

Romero simply continued the courageous reflective process initiated by his predecessor. Had he done otherwise, he would have been opposed very strongly by his clergy in the capital — many of whom had been persecuted by the authorities and tortured for their beliefs.

Like many of his episcopal colleagues from Latin America, Romero's position in Salvador was weakened by the degree of confusion which existed in some Vatican congregations concerning his actions and attitudes towards politics. The Archbishop seems to have developed the reputation for being a "troublesome monk.". He was not helped, of course, by the reports from many of his fellow bishops who were radically opposed to his form of social Christianity. During a synod of bishops, an intervention was made by one Salvadorean to the effect that catechists had been turned into secular revolutionaries. The image of a Church immersed in politics was not an uncommon view of Salvador in certain Roman quarters. Only Rivera Damas defended Romero when in Italy.

The Romero appointment to Salvador had really not been that controversial. If anything, he had been selected for his moderation in the face of strong nominations from the right and the moderate left. His subsequent "development" was a source of considerable surprise in Rome. However, it was not so much that the archbishop was particularly radical; it was more a question of the extremist nature of the social and political situation in his country.

Considerable blame for the misunderstanding of Romero in some Vatican congregations must rest with the failure of the local Papal Nuncio, Mgr Gerada, to come to terms with the problems facing the Salvadorean Church. In mitigation, he was not a permanent resident in Salvador. The nunciature, in the Escalón district of the capital, lay deserted for much of the year. Mgr Gerada spent most of his time in Guatemala City where he was on very close terms with Cardinal Mario Casariego, a man not known as a prominent admirer of Romero. It is clear, therefore, that the view of the "radical" Salvadorean Church from Guatemala City could be quite distorted on occasions. There is a saying in Salvador that if one is out of the country for an hour it takes a week to understand what has been happening. And if one is abroad for much longer, particularly in the controlled political environment of Guatemala, the task of analysis and reporting becomes all the more difficult.

Many members of the clergy felt that the nuncio was completely out of touch with the situation. He was also alleged to have been personally quite hostile to the archbishop. On one occasion, an Irish missionary nun, Sr Anselm, admonished him that he should get out and met the ordinary people.[20] His reply was to slam the table with his fist and demand petulantly whether he was expected to travel around by mule, to remote villages. Yes, she answered. It was obvious that two radically different pictures emerged of the country from the diplomatic cocktail circuit of the capital and the sherry-less *campesino* circuit.

But there were also other sources, besides the nuncio, presenting negative descriptions in Rome of Archbishop Romero and his work. The American and Salvadorean missions to the Holy See had the opportunity to make representations on behalf of their respective governments. But if the archbishop's prosecutors were plentiful, how powerful were his defenders? The answer was that since 1977, Romero was not without his powerful friends and admirers.

Romero had an opportunity to speak frankly to Pope Paul VI in the summer of 1978, when he went to Rome on his *ad limina* visit. There was no misunderstanding at that level. The problems were with members of some congregations, who were not as well versed as the elderly Pope with international affairs. Moreover, the much respected Provincial of the Jesuits in Central America, Fr Cesar Jerez, — who had not dis-similar problems to those of Romero — was in a position to inform his Superior General, Fr Arrupe, of the true situation in Salvador. At least, if confused, critical reports about Romero were reaching Rome all the time about the actions and ideas of the archbishop, there were those in residence who could put the other side.

In the short pontificate of John Paul I, there was no time to clear up existing misunderstandings. But when John Paul II took over the chair of St Peter, the Archbishop of San Salvador was in a strong position. Cardinal Aloisio Lorscheider of Brazil, who is credited with first singling out Cardinal Wojtyla at the conclave, visited Salvador to report on the situation. He was a man extremely well-equipped to assess the local situation. His experiences in Brazil were similar. The problems were identical. The psychology of conservatism the same.

Cardinal Lorscheider spent some time assessing the situation and then travelled to Rome where he filed a report which came down very heavily on the side of Monseñor Romero and was very critical of the opposition to him. The tables had been turned. Then in February, Romero travelled again to Europe where he received an honorary doctorate at Louvain. He also visited Rome where he was received in audience by Pope John Paul II. At that level anyway, there was no misunderstanding. And where else counted? But this is to leap ahead too fast. It is necessary to describe in some detail the unscrupulous campaign to defame Romero at home. Only then will it be possible to understand why the stance of the nuncio was so reprehensible.

Calumny from the Right: Marxnulfo Romero

Besides the pastoral on political organisations, Archbishop Romero issued three others, equally well thought out and important. But his determination to stick by the gospel of the poor, and to remain a firm defender of human rights in the face of tremendous criticism, won him the hatred of the right and the mistrust of most of his fellow bishops in El Salvador. One elderly Monseñor explained Archbishop Romero's position in a para-psychological way: He had known the entire family for a very long time indeed; they had all suffered from epilepsy, and that accounted for the archbishop's "strange" views. To another ecclesiastic he was the dupe of the Jesuits. And for the extreme right he was Oscar *Marxnulfo* Romero.

Perhaps the most extreme example of the propaganda launched against the archbishop by the right was the magazine *Opinion*, whose masthead claimed that it was the voice of the pueblo at the service of truth, and the defender of human rights. If it was that, then it had a very machiavellian way of showing it.

A cartoon showed two men in conversation:

—They say Monseñor Marxnulfo Romero is a politician.
—Go on, he is very religious.
—And how is that?
—Well, every Sunday he preaches religiously the hatred of the poor for the rich.[21]

Another cartoon showed a fierce looking catechist, gun in one hand, bible in the other, and hammer and sickle in his pocket. he is being told by Archbishop Romero: "How could they say you are guerrillas, my innocent little boys?" This cartoon had particularly sinister implications. In El Salvador, as the murdered Rutilio Grande commented not long before his death,

"It is practically illegal to be an authentic Christian."[23]

Apart from the effluent of the El Salvador gutter press, there were other signs that Romero's persistent and fearless denunciation of injustice was having some effect. One, showing a field full of crosses, carried the message: "This is the promised land which the terrorists offer us." The advertisement called for "a national antiterrorist crusade." Another advertisement showed a hammer and sickle on a wall with the words, "This is the cross of those who say they are our redeemers."[24]

Was there any truth in the allegations of the anti-Romero propaganda campaign? The clearest refutation of such slanders can be found in the archbishop's final pastoral letter *Mision de la Iglesia en Medio de la Crisis del Pais* which was issued in August, 1979. The document was characterised by the archbishop's usual clarity and simplicity; he addressed himself to the problems facing the church firmly and courageously. Romero selected three "idolatries" for special exposition: the absolutisation of wealth, which lays emphasis on "having more", and not on "being more" which ought to be the ideal motivating human progress: the absolutisation of the idea of private property, when the wealth of the few increases while the poverty of the masses worsens; finally, the idolatry of political power which conspired with the other two to form the root of structural and repressive violence — in the main the cause of Salvadorean economic, social and political underdevelopment: "Puebla, following the magisterium of the last popes and Medellín, condemns capitalism."[25]

Romero went on to condemn the doctrine of national security which "places the individual at the total disposal of the state, denies him any political rights and creates inequality in the fruits of development." The *pueblo* is subject to the tutelage of military and political elites who exploit anyone who opposes them, in the name of total war. The armed forces are entrusted to guard the present economic and political structure under the pretext that it is in the interest of national security. All those who are not in accord with the State are declared

78

enemies of the country. And because of that "national security" many assassinations, disappearances, arbitrary arrests, acts of terrorism, kidnappings and tortures are justified with total disrespect for the dignity of the human person.

While the archbishop dealt with the various types of violence — as he did in his third pastoral — he also outlined his own thinking on Marxism. Understood as an atheistic philosophy, it has to be rejected by the Christian, he argued. But Marxism can also be understood in another sense, as a scientific analysis of society and economy. Thus it is used by many in Latin America without prejudice to their religious principles. But Romero warned clearly about the dangers of such an approach while he maintained the validity of the distinction.

The propaganda of the anti-Romero campaign depicting the archbishop as a crude Marxist was quite unfounded. But that did not deter his detractors. They remained convinced that he was a "marxist" who was trying to compromise the independence of the Church by involving it in politics. The truth was that the archbishop had been quite ruthless about maintaining his independence from the various political interest groups in the country. That line of argument did not endear him on occasions to some of the very radical priets who felt that the Church had to identify itself with the left. The archbishop never allowed himself to be placed in a compromising position, even by the reckless action of some of his priests.

But no matter how much trouble Romero took to ensure that his own personal position would not be misunderstood, it had little effect on his many enemies. They believed what they liked. And that was most damaging to the prelate. It placed him under considerable pressure and the campaign against him was sustained and professionally organised.

If Romero refused to immerse the Salvadorean Church in partisan politics, there was little doubt where the archbishop stood as a critic of the feudal structure of his country. He committed the Church to the defence of the poor and to the transformation of the social, economic and political structures of the national security state. "We cannot speak of a politicised mission but of a mission that has to direct Christian consciences in a political milieu. Just as with every human activity, politics require a pastoral orientation. Our situation becomes grave when many Christians living in such a political milieu as exists in this country, take up a political position before they have found their Christian identity."[26]

Judging by the hysteria of the right and the expense which wealthy people obviously felt it necessary to go to, Archbishop Romero's message was obviously talking effect. The man who had gone from a remote diocese to take over the metropolitan see of San Salvador was obviously making his presence felt. Romero was never radical in a doctrinal sense; neither was he noted for his liberal attitude towards his clergy when bishop of Santiago de Maria. It was said that he wanted to be the parish priest wherever he controlled. But his move to the capital coincided with an escalation in political repression throughout the country in 1977. The murder of Rutilio Grande, one of the most respected intellectuals and pastors in the country, seemed to have been intellectually and spiritually quite decisive.

Archbishop Romero gradually began to change. He became much more open and receptive to new ideas. His long-standing concept of hierarchy in his attitude towards the clergy seemed to evaporate. Besides, he had much more in common with his priests than he had with all but one of the Salvadorean bishops. The future of the Salvadorean Church lay with the commitment, dedication and altruism of the ordinary clergy. In a manner of speaking, the bishops were beyond redemption. With the exception of Rivera Damas, the others thought that Romero had taken leave of his senses.

Not even the violence against the clergy in 1977 could bring the hierarchy together. Romero was practically on his own.

Chapter Three

PERSECUTION
THE PREFERENTIAL OPTION OF THE RADICAL RIGHT

I come to sing you a sad tale,
not even the bullets can silence me;
Monsenor Romero has fallen,
and his body, stretched on the floor,
arouses the people who begin to shout;

We've had enough, we've had enough,
we've had enough of death and falsehood.
We've had enough, we've had enough,
is the cry of El Salvador.

Three years he spent
fearlessly preaching justice and love,
defender of the poor and the humble
who suffer at the hand of the exploiter,
voice of the men without voice,
voice of the people of El Salvador.

Adapted from the song *Basta Ya*.

    Archbishop Romero knew that there was always the possibility that he might be murdered. He received death threats frequently. But he refused all forms of protection, and did not even bother to vary his daily routes. He was a prime target. Yet he argued that the poor people of the country, whom he represented, went without protection, then why should he be any different? The courage of the man will perhaps be a little more strongly appreciated when one looks at the number of priests who have died in El Salvador since 1977. The Jesuit, Routilio Grande as the first. But others followed quickly. On the same day that Fr Grande was killed, March 12, 1977, Manuel Barahona was shot dead at the wheel of his brother's car in San Juan Tepezontes. The gunmen had obviously mistaken Manuel for his brother, Fr Rafael. On May 1, Fr Jorge Sarsanedas, a Jesuit from Panama, was expelled after spending five days in prison on the grounds that he had a long record as a "subversive."

On May 5, 1977, a bomb damaged the printing works of *Orientación*. Six days later following the discovery of the body of the Foreign Minister, Borgonovo, who had been kidnapped by the left some time earlier, the White Warriors Union shot Fr Alfonso Navarro as a reprisal. A young boy also died in the attack.[1] Fr Navarro's final words were: "I die for preaching the gospel. I know who the perpetrators of my death are. May they know they are forgiven."[2] While the torture, beatings and expulsions continued, the national press carried numerous adverts from such groups as the Catholic Religious Women's Association; the Followers of Christ the King, etc., all fabricated for the occasion of putting in the articles.[3]

As the threats against the lives of priests continued into 1977, the auxiliary bishop of San Salvador, Mgr Arturo Rivera Damas, went into hiding. He had been repeatedly threatened by the right.[4] Many priests, too, were in much the same position. They could not live in their parishes. Some lived in the national seminary or stayed with friends. Each day they varied their routes and travelled as often as possible by the crowded public transport system in order to avoid the vegeance of the right. Then, on July 21, 1977, the White Warriors Union gave the forty seven Jesuits in the country an ultimatum to leave or face "execution." But they chose to remain and were not harmed.

Other clerics were less fortunate. Alfonso Navarro has already been mentioned. Fr Ernesto Barrera died with a number of youths allegedly in a shootout with the security forces. The military claimed that they had been engaged in a protracted gun battle. But other sources maintain that the people had been killed first and then a mock confrontation staged. The murdered priest was laid out in the road still "clutching" a revolver.[5]

The next killing of a priest was yet another case of a bogus confrontation. On Saturday, January 20, 1979, the national guard burst into the parochial compound of San Antonio Abad, outside San Salvador, at 06.00, and murdered the priest, Octavio Ortiz Luna (aged 34), and four youths, some of whom were minors. There was evidently no provocation. There was no evidence that the security forces tried to effect a peaceful entry.

The suggested motive for the killing of Octavio Ortiz is particularly pernicious. The relationship between Ortiz and the archbishop was very close.

Octavio Ortiz was an exceptionally successful priest. He was spiritual director at the minor seminary and he was also very active on a number of important ecclesiatical commissions.

He had spent the day before his death with Archbishop Romero working on projects of mutual interest. Fr Ortiz died because it was a way of getting at Romero and extending a warning.

The killings even shocked a country where such violence is a common-place. And in an article entitled "Basta Ya" in *Orientación*, the anger of the church was poured out:

> This tragic and unjust situation forces us to shout with our Archbishop, ENOUGH. Enough of blood and assassination, enough of violence, enough of kidnappings and guerrillas, an end to repression . . . . In no way do we want vengeance; we only ask for some justice that will awaken the hope of the *pueblo*, a hope that — by non-violent means — will bring the day when one can enjoy openly human rights and the rights of the children of God. May no lie or calumny sully the bloody but pure sacrifice of these new Salvadorean martyrs.[6]

Although *enough*, or "Basta Ya", became the slogan of defiance in Salvador, there was no let-up in the violence. The repression was unrelenting. Yet Archbishop Romero had little alternative but to carry on as before despite the draconian warning administered to him by the radical right in the killing of Octavio Ortiz. There was the conference of Latin American bishops to prepare for in Puebla. Few prelates went as well briefed or with as much enthusiasm as Archbishop Romero.

Sampling the Faith

Despite the intensive violence in Salvador, Romero found time to find out as accurately as possible the issues troubling the people in his archdiocese, so that he would be in a stronger position to speak out at Puebla. With the help of a priest sociologist, he issued a questionnaire which produced some very interesting results.[7] It was clear that the Medellin pledge on the "preferential option for the poor" remained a preoccupation with many Salvadorean Christians. But of the 106-strong sample, 104 (98.1%) felt that only a section of the Church had put that principle into practice. Thirty-two per cent thought that not all the members of the clergy and hierarchy were ready to take risks, hence there was a lack of unity among them. Eighteen per cent felt that some bishops and priests were afraid of persecution and preferred a quiet life, while 11% were of the opinion that clergy feared a loss of privilege. A further 8.2% felt that "there is bad in some members of the hierarchy who refuse to read the signs of the times." There was strong support for the development of the teachings of Medellin.

To the question about which sector of Christian life was most opposed to the pastoral action inspired by Medellin, 106 people gave 488 different answers; 100 mentioned the Salvadorean businessmen association (ANEP); 92 referred to the Salvadorean Landowner

Association (FARO); 82 mentioned the government; 60 spoke of the bishops of Santa Ana, San Miguel, and San Vicente; and 41 mentioned a small group of priests siding with the government and or with the rich. 25 of the answers referred to the Papal Nuncio, another 36 to ORDEN and 12 referred to some popular movements of Marxist tendency while 11 mentioned the mass communications media.

One hundred out of 106 answered Yes to the question whether Puebla should confirm the teachings of Medellin. They stressed that the bishops should take into account the experience of martyrdom in the Church in Latin America, and should solemnly commit themselves to the poor.

Seventy-two per cent of those who replied felt that there were but few possibilities of total evangelisation of the human person within the capitalist system. Most suggested that this was because capitalists "provoke repression" or "do not allow democratic freedoms" or "close their eyes to injustices." Other reasons put forward were: "because it is fundamentally a materialistic system"; "because the system dominates the church"; "because it is a system which is radically opposed to the spirit of the Gospel"; "because the church does not want to lose the privileges of the system"; "because the system buys the communication media and distorts the truth."

Others, not quite as pessimistic, felt that there were many possibilities of evangelisation even within the capitalist system. These possibilities depended "on the condition that the conscientisation work increases" or on "the condition that they distribute their goods." Further reasons were given for optimism: "the experience of martyrdom may convert them"; "there is good will also among them"; "if they come to agreement with the church"; "the majority are poor and at the end will convert them"; "because love is strong."

Armed with his own profound pastoral experience, distraught at the death of his close friend, Fr Octavio Ortiz, and carrying the results of his survey, Archbishop

Romero set off for Mexico to attend CELAM III[8] towards the end of January 1979.

Pope John Paul II travelled to Puebla to open the conference and delivered a sermon from which many conservative prelates took false solace. But the January 28 address ought to be read in conjunction with the general audience address on February 21, 1979. It has to be concluded that the then new Pope was very much aware of the complexity and richness of the thinking within a divided Latin American church. Although John Paul II admonished priests not to become involved in politics, that did not mean he was excluding a theology based on the "preferential option for the poor."

Archbishop Romero was slightly bemused and not a little displeased by what he experienced at Puebla. Some of his closest friends, many of whom had come expressly with the archbishop to advise him, were excluded from the main conference. Instead, the "liberation" theologians conducted a series of evening seminars outside the assembly hall while Archbishop Romero, supported by many other episcopal colleagues, attempted to incorporate certain progressive ideas into the final documents. There was a bitter struggle to prevent the clock being turned back on Medellin. Discussions were often heated, as when one bishop remarked pointing to those who were scandalised by the possible use of certain Marxist ideas by Christians: "Let him who is without an ideology cast the first stone." The theology of liberation had not so much drawn the church into conflict with repressive regimes as made explicit the radically un-Christian basis of liberal capitalist society, and the national security state. Therefore Christians could no longer remain passively loyal citizens in dictatorships where the poor were mercilessly exploited and persecuted.

Unfortunately, opposition to the Church of the poor did not just come from the civil authorities. According to the theologian, Jon Sobrino, "some nuncios and members of the hierarchy who were anxious to get back to less tense and more diplomatic approaches" were prepared to compromise. Romero fought very hard against such an eventuality at Puebla. There was no going back for the church in Latin America. But the struggle was by no means an easy one for the Archbishop of Salvador. At the end of the day, he and his allies had made a major impression on the content of the documents. But their victory was far from decisive. They really prevented a reversal rather than won an advance.[9] Romero had good reason to be pleased with the outcome; the teachings of Medellin had made such an impact that ten years afterwards it proved impossible to manoeuvre the Latin American church into a U-turn.

But no matter how disappointing Puebla proved for some, it ended in something of a personal victory for Romero. During a press conference, the archbishop was given a standing ovation by the journalists present— acclaim hard-wrung and stintingly given from such a hard-bitten lot. He related the news from Salvador that a rightwing group had put out a contract on his life. He spoke of taking reasonable precautions as a result of the opposition to his preaching. But he didn't overdo it because he felt that everyone was in the hands of God: "to know one has died fulfilling his vocation, his duty, that is a victory, a triumph," he added. "I will stay with my people", he concluded.

Under sentence of death

At Puebla Archbishop Romero had seen pettiness, personal rivalry among his brother bishops, and occasional unedifying exchanges on the floor of the conference. Certain Mexican newspapers had carried out a systematic campaign to call into question the motives of many of the liberation theologians who had gathered in Puebla only to be excluded from the proceedings. In other words, CELAM III was very much like home for Archbishop Romero. Yet despite his mixed feelings, the final documents reflected the preoccupations of the

Romero questionnaire. The preferential option for the poor had been defended successfully.

Under "sentence" of death from a number of right-wing groups, the archbishop went about his normal work with continued vigour and equanimity. But the violence against the church of the poor continued unabated. In June, 1979, Fr Rafeal Palacios was shot as he went to his car in Santa Tecla by the White Warriors Union, allegedly in reprisal for a leftwing killing of a local army officer. Outside the diocese of San Salvador, another priest died on August 4; Fr. Alirio Napoleon Macias was taken from his church in the diocese of San Vicente and shot by assailants unknown.

All the murdered priests had one striking feature in common. They were very close to Archbishop Romero and strong defenders of the "preferential option for the poor." Such men have been depicted as being something of a revolutionary minority. The Archbishop was described as an agent of division and the leader of a clerical faction. But the compromise Puebla document clearly gave weight to the Archbishop of Salvador's position. Romero was in the mainstream of Catholic social teaching. His critics and opponents had been left far behind by recent pastoral developments. Some Salvadorean bishops remained encrusted in the inglorious clerical past—the church of profound social divisions and class conflict.

Romero, in contrast, energised the local church building upon the strong pastoral base laid by his predecessor in the archdiocese, Monsenor Luis Chavez y Gonzalez. Both men had brought the ordinary people into much closer communion with the ecclesiastical authorities. Religion was shown to be relevant to the social conditions of the poor, the emarginated and the outcasts. Christianity had the power to transform the wretched into an *anawim,* the followers of the "God of the weathered features who sweats in the street."

Archbishop Romero was not only listened to in the shanty towns or in the wattle huts of the campesinos. The intellectuals and the middle classes also found his words challenging. He was not the agent of a class-based religion as his detractors used to repeat *ad nauseam*. On the contrary, he was very much a believer in dialogue, even at times when the application of that philosophy of open administration resulted in abuse, endless irritation and torrents of the most uncharitable criticism. But when the irrational aspect of administration got too much for him, Romero took refuge in the company of the slum dwellers and the poor campesinos. Whatever self-doubt might have been provoked by the wranglings of national episcopal conferences quickly evaporated when he relaxed with his people in their wretched surroundings. Recharged by his experiences in the slums, he could come back to his desk at the archepiscopacy rid of any doubts about the validity of a theology which took the poor as a starting point.

Romero also gave the lie to the calumny that his conception of the preferential option for the poor was class-based. The archbishop was always very active in trying to secure the release of rich kidnap victims. On one occasion, Jon Sobrino recalls how the archbishop had intervened successfully. It was obvious that the wealthy family members did not like the archbishop very much. But when "they talked to him they were impressed by his humanity and by his friendliness."[10]

In other words, Romero did not divide the church. But his episcopal and clerical colleagues did so by not keeping pace with developments in Catholic social teaching. The archbishop was, in fact, partially responsible for the religious revival taking place in Salvador. He made no apology for his love of the poor. They were his refuge and his strength.

No matter how difficult his tasks, he could always derive the most profound satisfaction from talking and dialoguing with the poor, who proved to be much more open than many clergy. "You know, he had problems with everybody," recalls Fr Sobrino. But he used to say that what really gave him "hope and strength" was talking with the ordinary people. He spent a lot of time in the small villages, presiding at fiestas, baptising, confirming and marrying people in the small make-shift straw-roofed chapels. He was a bishop in the tradition of Bartolome de las Casas and other New World prelates who earned the title "protector of the Indians." He was a defender of the poor.

Fearless preaching of justice

On February 10, 1980, Romero returned to Salvador after a trip to Europe where he had received an honorary doctorate from the University of Louvain. There he had taken the opportunity in his acceptance speech to tell the West about the political reality in Salvador where the October 15 coup had failed to halt the repression being carried out by the security forces and the right. He had travelled on to Rome, accompanied by the Provincial of the Jesuits, Fr Cesar Jerez. They met Pope John Paul II and Romero had an opportunity to give him a briefing on recent ecclesiastical and political developments in his country. The archbishop found the Pope a sympathetic listener. If sides had to be taken in Salvador, there was no doubt on which side Pope John Paul II stood. The early misunderstandings with certain Roman Congregations had been superseded by the close friendship between the archbishop and the Pope. It would prove much more difficult to misrepresent Romero at the Vatican in the future.[11]

The archbishop was no longer a minority voice in an obscure capital in a remote part of Central America. He was fast becoming a figure with growing international influence. That was one of the most dangerous features of the situation for the "parallel government" in Salvador.

On his return from Europe, Romero set about telling the country on February 10, in one of his famous Sunday sermons, how El Salvador was seen from Europe. The picture was not very flattering. In his two hour exposition, he moved to some theological reflections on God's call to "construct our history with Him." Finally, as was the usual practice, he spoke of "the facts of civil life in the country." There he revealed the catalogue of transgressions against human rights in Salvador during the previous week. He named names, dates and places. In a country where the press and other media are not free, he was a lone source of information. Yet it was the experience of actually hearing such unspeakable crimes being publicised which actually brought thousands flocking each Sunday to the cathedral. There people could experience the satisfaction of witnessing a courageous man flaunt the might of the national security state. Romero acted exactly as if he was living in a stable democracy where the most that could happen to him was the serving of a parking fine by a garrulous policeman. The cathedral on Sundays became an oasis of freedom and defiance for many who had to live their ordinary lives in fear and servitude. Romero's sermons were like some regular democratic pageant, a Brechtean play where catharsis came to a tormented audience. Romero condemned the actions of the security forces, the politicians and the extremists of both the right and the left with a calculated Christian recklessness. His analysis was penetrating, his facts were horrifyingly accurate and his message was being received by an increasing number of people.

Besides, the newspaper and radio station of the archdiocese used to carry his words to an even wider audience. Unfortunately, the range of the transmitter meant that his words did not travel quite as far as people would have liked. Moreover, the high illiteracy rate in the country, estimated among adults to be about 50%, restricted the impact of *Orientación*. But the magnetism of the man could not be contained by repression. He was a tireless traveller and was no stranger to the homes of the poor, where he insisted on sharing their humble meal rather than eating something prepared for him. But however effective Romero might have been in listing the number of "disappeared" people the real threat to the "parallel government" came when the reputation of the archbishop began to spread beyond the confines of his own country. He had caused acute embarrassment to the rightist groups by his Louvain address in early February. The Louvain address, and the *Prensa Latina* interview simply mirrored Romero's thinking as reflected in his Sunday sermons. There was one very significant advance. The archbishop's voice was being heard abroad, and that was of considerable concern to the "parallel government". Then on the seventeenth of February, Romero embarked on perhaps his most dangerous venture.

Arms embargo call to Washington

On February 17, 1980, the archbishop took the drastic step of writing an open letter to the American President, Jimmy Carter. He expressed concern over the reports that the United States was studying the way to favour the arms race in Salvador by sending military and advisory teams to "train three Salvadorean battalions in logistics, communications and intelligence." But the archbishop felt that such a move would only "sharpen the injustice and repression against the organised people who have been struggling many times that their fundamental human rights be respected. The junta had not shown a capacity to resolve grave national problems, resorting "to repressive violence producing many more deaths and injured than during the recent past military regimes" whose systematic violation of human rights was denounced by the inter-American Commission on Human Rights.

He added that it was obvious that "the junta and the Christian Democrats did not govern the country, but that political power is in the hand of military personnel without scruples, and the only thing that they know how to do is to repress the people and to favour the interests of the Salvadorean oligarchy". He cited reports that the Americans had supplied $200,000 worth of gas masks and other equipment to be used to break up demonstrations. He asked President Carter to prohibit military aid to the Salvadorean government and to guarantee that the U.S. would not intervene in any way in the internal affairs of Salvador. Archbishop Romero continued: "It would be unjust and deplorable that through the interference of foreign powers the Salvadorean people would be frustrated, repressed and impeded in deciding with autonomy the economic and political road which the country must follow." President Carter could hardly afford to ignore the voice of one who commanded such respect internationally—whatever logistical experts and geo-political strategists might say in the Pentagon. The fear of another Nicaragua was an over-riding consideration in U.S. military circles. But in Salvador, the genuine American attempts to force the junta to initiate social reform had met with very little success. The "parallel government" was far too strong and was in a position to veto practically every move made by the legitimate authorities.

Curiously, from the realms of comparative obscurity, the country of Salvador had begun to take on considerable importance at the State Department. One well placed ecclesiastical source said that at one point it had become second only to Iran. Without any doubt, a major U.S. effort was being made to effect radical change which might in turn produce the economic and social stability which would be conducive to creating conditions of political equilibrium. If the policy succeeded, America would be regarded as the architect of progress in Salvador—an image which would stand in contrast to the more popular Latin American stereotype of the ugly American.

In fact on February 23, a State Department spokesman said that the then Secretary of State, Mr. Cyrus Vance, had warned the junta through the ambassador that support for the government was conditional upon local commitment to human rights and general reform. The message added that although the U.S. was opposed to changing the government, aid would be cut off if the government did not continue to contain civilians or committed abuses against human rights.

Clearly, the momentum for pursuing a policy of radical social reform in Salvador enjoyed considerable support within the State Department. Cyrus Vance was a very strong advocate of a foreign policy based on human rights. As a result, the appeal from Romero was of considerable importance. It carried weight. If anyone in Salvador had the authority and international prestige to influence the White House and the State Department, it was the Nobel Prize nominee, Oscar Romero. However, it is very doubtful that he would have been able to effect a major policy change by himself. But he knew that he would be listened to and his opinions would be treated with some seriousness.

As such he posed a major threat to the "parallel government"; and as his international reputation and prestige grew, so too did the danger to the undemocratic military/oligarchy alliance which was responsible for neutralising the reform programme of the legitimate government and causing so much indiscriminate violence and repression in the country. The Salvador/Washington axis was of cardinal importance to the continued repressive efficiency of the "parallel" rightist forces. It suited that coalition not to topple the junta and its ineffectual government; to do so would have resulted in an immediate cessation of U.S. aid. In those circumstances, the rightist forces enjoyed the best of both worlds; that amorphous, faceless group could remain in the shadows, control the country and at the same time enjoy the benefits of U.S. aid which was being paid to a government that did not really have control. They were a front; but many of its members sincerely believed that no matter how ineffectual they might be in office, it was better for them to remain rather than to hand the government over to the security forces who would carry out the bidding of the "parallel government" with even more ruthlessness.

Romero threatened that fragile political structure more than any other individual. His open letter to

President Carter was an act of considerable defiance which went to the very heart of the Salvadorean problem. The archbishop could preach as openly as he wished inside the country where the rightist forces were very much in the ascendant. He could expose details of the repression, the violence and the intimidation. But like his ecclesiastical colleagues, the archbishop could only rely on the moral force of his argument. His rightist opponents could depend upon force of arms. But when Romero appealed to Carter directly he had taken his opposition onto a much more dangerous level which was compounded by his growing international reputation as a campaigner for human rights.

The day after Romero sent his letter to Carter, the diocesan radio station in the capital was blown up. An unsuccessful attempt had been made earlier in the year. The second attack wrecked the entire station which is situated in the national seminary.[12]

Undeterred, he preached as usual in the cathedral on the following Sunday. The archbishop read out the letter he had written to Washington. He addressed himself then to the Christian Democrats and said that by their continued presence in government they were concealing the repressive character of the regime from the outside world. He still felt that there were some good men in the military. But, because of the repression, he said, there was the impression that it was the right who were in control. He spoke of the persistent rumours which hinted at connivance between the security forces and the clandestine armed groups on the right.

It appeared that the greater the threat to his life, the more reckless he became in his preaching and actions. Many friends prevailed upon him to travel only in the company of an armed bodyguard. But he declined to accept even minimal protection. His argument was devastatingly simple: He repeatedly countered the anxious protestations of friends about his vulnerability by saying that the ordinary campesino had no protection and he too was one of the poor. However, he was persuaded to vary his route as much as possible. But the arrival of an archbishop in a slum or village was a matter of some publicity. If Mass, marriages, confirmations and baptisms were scheduled for the evening, then the archbishop would never agree to alter a time for reasons of personal safety.

There was no bravado in his actions. It was very obvious that the campaign of villification and calumny against Romero had given way to a ruthless plan to kill the archbishop. In early March, over seventy sticks of gelignite had been found primed to go off in the basilica of the Sagrada Corazon at a time when the archbishop was preaching his Sunday sermon. There may have been other unpublished attempts on his life.

On March 23, he preached what was to be his final sermon in the same basilica where the gelignite had been found two weeks earlier. It was to be one of his strongest statements on political repression, and his appeal was directly to the security forces:

> "Brothers, you are from our same pueblo, you kill our brother campesinos; and before an order to kill given by a man you ought to reflect on the law of God which says: do not kill. No soldier is obliged to obey an order that is contrary to the law of God. Nobody has to fulfil an immoral law. Now it is time that you recover your consciences and that you first obey your conscience than an order to sin. The Church, defender of the rights of God, of the law of God, of the human dignity of the person, cannot remain shut up before such an abomination. We want the government to take seriously that reforms achieved with so much blood serve no one. In the name of God, then, and in the name of this suffering pueblo, whose cries rise to the heavens, every day more clamouringly, I beg, I ask, I order you in the name of God: stop the repression."[13]

These words were seen as a final act of defiance. The appeal was seen as an act of sedition. The armed forces spokesman, Col. Marco Aurelio Gonzalez, described the sentiments expressed in the sermon as "criminal".

After that Sunday, the archbishop had even fewer friends. He had alienated the military by his appeal to disobedience and he had given an even greater sense of urgency to the para-military rightist forces operating under the aegis of the "parallel government" to execute the long-standing death threat against the archbishop. Plans had been laid carefully. It was now a question of accelerating the implementation of the scheme. A professional killer, a jackal, was already in the country, according to some sources, and ready to fulfil his "contract".[14]

On July 8, 1979 Archbishop Romero had preached one of his most celebrated sermons on the theme, "the prophet, and the presence of God in society." He proposed a hypothesis which then seemed rather far fetched:

"Brothers, this morning I would like to appeal to that prophetic vocation which you all have. And I would like to say to you, as I once said to you before: If anytime they stop the radio, ban the papers, deny us the possibility of speaking, kill all the priests and the bishop too; and they leave yourselves, a pueblo without priests, everyone of us must be a microphone of God; every one of you must be a messenger, a prophet; the Church will always exist in the world for as long as there remains one baptised person and that last baptised person who remains in the world, it is he who has before the entire world the responsibility to maintain the flag of Our Lord's truth and Divine Justice flying high."

Such an apocalyptical vision may read a little strangely to those who did not know Salvador as well as the archbishop did. By March, 1980, less than eight months after that sermon, about 1,000 people had died in political violence, priests and catechists were persecuted, and the radio had been silenced. The most articulate opponents of the "parallel government" were being either killed, "disappeared", tortured, imprisoned, intimidated or forced into exile. The man who was spearheading that opposition was Archbishop Romero, and his reckless courage had begun to win headlines and friends abroad. His best friends had been murdered, but he had refused to keep his silence. Some of the most idealistic Salvadoreans of his generation had been forced into political exile. He refused to follow them. A sophisticated campaign of character assassination had also failed to destroy his effectiveness. He could not be frightened by death threats. Therefore, the "parallel government" had no alternative but to kill him. There was no room for failure; so a "jackal" was brought from abroad and ordered to carry out his task without delay.

Chapter Four

MURDER AT THE CATHEDRAL

My job seems to be to go around picking up insults
and corpses.

Archbishop Romero, quoted by Jon Sobrino.

Most Europeans did not become aware of the murder
of Archbishop Romero until early on Tuesday morning,
March 25, 1980. The news was sickening. The circumstances of the murder were appalling. The archbishop
had chosen to live in a cancer hospital, in the Colonia
Miramonte, San Salvador. He used to say Mass regularly for patients in the small chapel of the Divine
Providence hospital. That particular day he was offering
Mass for the mother of a newspaper publisher, Senor
Jorge Pinto. The family had placed an advertisement in
the press giving the time of the service and the name of
the celebrant.

Just after the archbishop finished the Liturgy of the
Word, during which he had spoken about the triumph
of the Resurrection over death, four men entered the
church and one fired a rifle shot from about thirty
metres. Reports are quite confused. One eye-witness
spoke of several shots being fired while the Vicar General, Monsenor Urioste, said that a single bullet struck
the archbishop[1]. Romero died instantly as the high
velocity shot cut through an artery to the heart. The
assailants made their getaway in the chaos which
followed,

It was strange that the killers chose such a public
occasion for their crime. But the extreme right, who
must take full responsibility for the murder, have a

rather sophisticated and profane sense of timing in Salvador. The archbishop could more easily have been attacked on a lonely country road as he returned alone from an out-lying village. But the assassination was carried out during a Mass with a small congregation present. The action was calculated to maximise the terrorist impact on the Salvadorean people. Romero had received many death threats. He knew that he was top of the notorious 'list' in the capital and that did not seem to worry him. He possessed a certain serenity which characterised his stance in the face of so much danger.

That Cuban connection

Romero was murdered because he loved the poor and considered the struggle for justice an integral part of faith. Although nobody has taken responsibility, it is possible to ask: Who has been killing priests in Salvador? Who had threatened the life of Romero? Who had ordered the Jesuits to quit the country or face the same fate as Rutilio Grande? The answer in all cases was the para-military right and the Union Guerrero Blanco (UGB) in particular, the agents of the "parallel government."

In the last weeks of his life, Romero had acted in a particularly provocative way by writing to President Carter calling for an arms embargo which, if implemented, would have eventually crippled the military and the oligarchy. The real possibility that Romero might get through to Carter was the cause of gravest concern in the cuarteles and latifundios of El Salvador. The appeal to soldiers to stop the repression and, if necessary, disobey orders from superiors when there was a clear question of conscience at stake, did little to enhance the archbishop's reputation with the military.

But it was Romero's threat in the international sphere, where the archbishop stood to win a Nobel peace prize, that was the cause of most concern to the "parallel government". The repression could continue as long as the regime had sufficient international credibility to function effectively. Romero threatened the oligarchy's future. He stood to undermine military links with Washington. Finally, the sermons were a constant source of offence to the right who had details of repression and killings publicly denounced from the altar in the capital with fearless regularity. Therefore, his continued earthly presence was no longer desirable.

The interesting feature of Romero's assassination, is the widespread belief among well-informed Salvadorean ecclesiastics, that the killing was not a haphazard "hit and run" affair. US embassy sources in Salvador also indicated that the killer was a marksman who had taken up a good shooting position outside the church. The newly appointed ambassador from Washington, Mr Robert White, suggested that right-wing Cuban exiles had been involved. There appeared to be some connection between the murder of the archbishop and the killing of a prominent Chilean exile in Washington four years earlier. See Epilogue.

On September 21, 1976, Orlando Letelier, who had served as Minister of Defence in the government of Salvador Allende, was driving from his home in Washington where he was spearheading an international campaign against the regime of Pinochet. He had been deprived of his Chilean citizenship a few days before a bomb exploded under his car killing the general instantly; and his death deprived the followers of the murdered Allende of one of the foremost Chilean politicians and intellectuals.

The *Washington Post* on February 1, 1976, blamed the paramilitary Cuban exile Brigade 2505 for the murder; the right-wing group formed part of the wider United Revolution Organisation Co-ordination (CORU). It offered its specialist services to repressive regimes or to "parallel governments" to rid the world of liberal people likely to cause problems for right-wing juntas either at home or abroad. Elements in Salvador availed of such expertise. Two men, wanted for questioning in connection with the Letelier murder, were reported to have been seen in San Salvador a few days before the killing of the archbishop. Although the murderers of the archbishop have never been found, and no one has come forward to accept responsibility, the theory about Cuban exile involvement at the behest of the Salvadorean "parallel government" has grown in strength.

The theory was certainly aired among the clergy and other sources in Salvador in the weeks following the murder. The killing was different from many others. Of course, there was no shortage of expertise within the country. Murder squads have had plenty of practice in Salvador. Right wing fringe groups abound. But the idea of a maverick murder-gang taking the law into their own hands and setting out to kill the archbishop, as ordinary Salvadoreans are done away with regularly, has been discounted by many clergy. It is considered most unlikely that an autonomous group engineered the attack. Many have equally ruled out the possibility of direct involvement by UGB paramilitaries.

Romero was not the only bishop to be threatened in Salvador. His episcopal colleague and ally, Monsenor Rivera Damas, had also received numerous death threats, and at one stage, while auxiliary bishop of the capital, he was forced to go into hiding. He had no doubt in blaming the extreme right for the numerous menacing letters and the attack on his catechetical centre.[2] But that was in the early 1970s. Ten years later, the right were much better organised. So much so that it was possible to talk about a "parallel government." Romero's successor expressed the majority ecclesiastical view that the archbishop was killed because he loved the poor. The motive was much easier to establish than it was to find the culprits.

The *Times* summed up, in an editorial, the real reason for Romero's death; he was "killed because he had become a symbol — of the need for human rights and social justice . . . obviously he was a thorn in the side of successive governments, and particularly resented by the armed forces."[3] He was a martyr for the poor.

As news of the murder was flashed around the world, condemnations began to flow into the national seminary where Romero had had his office. The junta declared three days of mourning over "the most vile of crimes,"[4] and reiterated their firm intention to stop the terrorism. For once the Salvadorean hierarchy were united in their condemnation; they excommunicated the guilty and praised the work of Romero as a man "who remained faithful to his motto of speaking the truth in an effort to construct fundamental peace in justice." The statement continued that he "announced the Message of Salvation without flagging and he denounced with implacable vigour institutionalised injustice and abuses against human rights and the inalienable dignity of man, made in the image and likeness of God."[5] The poor of the country were stunned. They had another martyr. But they had lost a fearless champion.

Encounter with the national security state

After a 24-hour plane journey, I arrived in San Salvador to cover the archbishop's funeral for RTE, Irish radio and television, on Friday 28 March, 1980. Then it was a two-hour drive into the capital past the familiar Latin American sights of a procession of people carrying enormous loads for miles in the heat. Beasts of burden, no more.

The houses we passed were built with sticks, mud and cardboard. The primitive accommodation—like a furnace in summer and a sieve in the wet, winter season —stands in marked contrast to the obscenely modern automatic weapons in the possession of the security forces who are everywhere, the best that American money can buy and supply.

The cathedral of San Salvador in the heart of the city showed all the signs of continued siege. There was evidence of bombing while the larger department stores—air-conditioned of course—have long since bricked up all their large display windows. In the midst of gloom stands the cathedral, crowned with a huge dome and looking as if it had never quite been finished, a symbol or relic of a concept of the church as an institution which has faded from fashion in Central America. Inside, sunlight streams through the many bullet holes over the huge front door. The furnishings were rather simple. A few benches, a number of side altars, a picture of Our Lady of Guadelupe, and a baroque statue of the Sacred Heart. There were two other large entrances at either side of the main altar behind which gaudy electric light bulbs lit up in the shape of a cross.

In such surroundings Archbishop Romero used to preach his famous sermon each Sunday, that is, when the cathedral was not being occupied by one popular organisation or another.

That Friday, the murdered archbishop lay before the high altar in a glass-topped coffin surrounded by lighted candles. Outside there were no police or military in sight, an unusual occurrence in a national security state such as Salvador. It was as if a small republic had been declared in the very heart of the capital. Boy scouts were on crowd-control duty. Hundreds of people had come from the country to pay their last respects to the archbishop. Two lines formed in the blazing sun—men on one side, women on the other—waiting their turn to file past the coffin. Security was particularly tight; and youths who seemed to know their job searched everyone going into the cathedral. It was explained to me that they were trying to prevent bombs or explosives from being planted inside.

As people walked by the coffin, many stopped to touch it or press a picture of Romero to the glass, as if such a relic might be called upon in the near future to provide protection for the owner from danger. Mass was said each day at noon in a packed cathedral. That day it was the turn of the Provincial of the Jesuits in Central America, Fr Cesar Jerez, to preach. He is a most impressive speaker, an intellectual who could strike just the right tone. Romero was murdered, he said defiantly, simply because he loved the poor and fought for social justice. It was difficult to believe that such a simple statement of fact could sign a man's death warrant. But the evidence was to become compelling.

After the Mass, I met Gustavo Gutierrez, one of the foremost exponents of liberation theology, who is a secular priest in Lima. He was speaking to a group of priests, nuns and seminarians who were on hunger strike in protest at the killings. Many of those priests were, like Romero, on the death lists. In their Communique No. 2, the group said that neither Jesus nor Romero was mediocre. They denounced repression, and the hunger strikers intended to do the same. Therefore, they denounced before the Salvadorean people and the entire world that the killing of Romero was not an isolated incident but that it formed part of a widespread repression carried out by the armed forces. They also held responsible: American imperialism, the White Guerrillas and the O.L.C. "who are nothing more than the same 'security' forces dressed in civilian clothes and the armed forces," the oligarchy and their accomplices (the junta and the Christian Democrats) and the bishops who left Romero alone "and who calumniated him inside and outside the country." In the charged atmosphere of the cathedral measured statements could not be expected. For the hunger strikers, institutionalised violence was omnipresent. And that sense of urgency was in their statements.

Apart from the intense group of hunger-strikers, there was a sense of joy within the cathedral. A sense of relief might be more accurate. The Salvadorean Church felt that it was no longer alone in its hour of persecution and priests forgot the usual round of daily preoccupations with violence to throw themselves into the task of preparing for so many visitors. Salvadoreans no longer felt isolated. But the weeping of ordinary men and women as they passed the coffin of Romero brought one back to the reality of the national security state.

The following day, the cathedral was even more crowded at mid-day for Mass. The atmosphere was quite festive. But from a number of well informed sources I learned that a number of threats had already been received to disrupt the funeral service. Security was stepped up in an unobtrusive way. The cathedral was locked overnight. Only the hunger-strikers remained and the security personnel from the popular organisations.

Bishop Eamon Casey of Galway flew in next evening with an entire plane-load of people making their way to the funeral. Among the many clerics was Bishop James O'Brien of Westminster, a tall, thin, phlegmatic Englishman, who was to exhibit great coolness, courage and clear-headedness in the face of extraordinary pressure during the next two days. Beside Bishop O'Brien stood a Mexican, also tall, but bearded, wearing jeans, an old shirt and a sombrero round his neck. He was Fr Sanchez Sanchez, a worker-priest. Fr Gerry Moore and Fr Peter O'Neill from Gotera were there too. The Franciscans drove back to the convent where the English-speaking bishops were staying. Dr. Casey was very enthusiastic. He was anxious to explain that he had made the journey to represent the Irish hierarchy and he was in Salvador to show that the Irish Church cared, stood in solidarity with the principles for which Romero gave his life. The car sped through the darkness towards the capital past the shanty towns, and past the military patrols made all the more sinister by their furtiveness and the reputation they enjoyed for gratuitous violence. But with so many visiting dignitaries arriving that night, they were on their best behaviour.

The funeral

On Sunday morning, March 30, the sun shone brilliantly on a beautifully clear day. Our small group was joined by the other Franciscans from Gotera, Sisters Anselm, Jean, Rosemary and Fathers Ciaran Noonan and Alfred O'Loughlin.

At the Basilica of Sagrada Corazón, the church where some weeks earlier seventy sticks of gelignite had been found, primed to blow up during the sermon of the archbishop, an impressive number of bishops, priests and nuns were gathering to vest and walk in procession to the cathedral about half a mile away. It was Palm Sunday. The streets were surprisingly deserted. Although we did not realise it at the time, fear was keeping the ordinary people inside. They would not even come out to look at the procession of visiting dignitaries from all over the world.

Bishop Casey and the Foreign Minister of Nicaragua, Fr Miguel D'Escoto, headed the procession. The bishop was dressed entirely in red. He spoke animatedly to his priest politician partner. Many of the dignitaries carried palm.

As the file of priests moved off at a dignified pace down the hill, I walked ahead to catch a glimpse of the huge crowd that was expected to form in the Plaza Barrios before the cathedral. Passing by one side-street, I saw two national guards standing outside the Guatemalan embassy which had been attacked a few days earlier by leftwing militants. There was no evidence of a strong military presence in the city.

Near the cathedral, members of the popular organisations were assembling to march. Long pieces of red material were stretched out on the road as youths worked to cut out letters for their banners.

Suddenly, I walked from a deserted street and turned a corner into the main Plaza Barrios before the cathedral to find it thronged with enthusiastic, joyful people—an island of humanity in a deserted city. It seemed as if the entire capital had crowded into the compact square. But that was not the case. Thousands had made the pilgrimage from the countryside. The majority were campesinos who had come on foot, by lorry, and crowded bus to the city. They had made the pilgrimage from their villages at considerable personal risk. But fear kept many of the city people at home. They had seen what had happened to demonstrations in the past. The funeral of an archbishop did not necessarily enjoy immunity.

On that particular Sunday, the capital was divided into those who supported Romero, and those who did not. There were no detached or casual observers except for the press.

I showed my yellow press card, which had been issued by the archdiocese, and a boy scout let me through the cordon to the front of the huge, swaying crowd. The footpath in front of the cathedral steps, where an open-air altar had been erected, was reserved for journalists. The ten foot high iron railing gates were closed and locked. It was intended to place the coffin of the murdered archbishop between the altar and the iron gates before the start of the Mass. A choir, conducted by a very fat and popular composer, sang enthusiastically. There was a flurry of activity on the steps around the altar as a nervous master of ceremonies made sure that everything was ready. There was no obvious sense of danger as people busied themselves straightening the celebrant's chair and smoothing the altar linen.

In the square before the altar, about 100,000 people had gathered to form a huge congregation of Salvadorean poor. They clasped pictures of Romero, pieces of palm, radios and umbrellas which were used to protect the owners from the sweltering sun. An hour before the Mass began, the crush was particularly dangerous. There were no crowd barriers in the square. There were no policemen present to maintain order. That task was left to boy scouts who manfully tried to prevent the congregation from bursting through the single rope which separated the crowds from the thin strip of pavement before the cathedral railings. Children were fainting in the heat and were being passed over the heads of the crowd to the boy scouts in front followed by frantic parents who elbowed and jostled their way through the throngs so that they would not be separated from their family. In the ordinary course of events, it would have been difficult to maintain order. But if anything should happen to cause panic . . .

Looking around at the high buildings which closed in

the square on three sides, I reflected on the lack of
security and the obvious advantage offered to any group
who might like to attack the funeral. The Palacio
Nacional, to the right of the square, was strategically
placed as its flat roof offered a natural firing point for
snipers. It had been used for that purpose before. But
despite the rumours and threats I put the idea out of my
mind. For no clear reason, I made my way around the
side to the door of the cathedral where the procession
was just entering. Inside, hundreds of nuns dressed in
white stood along the main altar area. They had been
there for hours. And they prayed and sang and wept.

The catafalque was surrounded by candles. I was
introduced to the parents of Fr Ortiz — the priest who
had been murdered just before Archbishop Romero
had set out for Puebla. They were very ordinary country
people, much the same as the congregation outside.
And they were not bitter about what had happened to
their son. They combined a certain fatalism with hope,
a Christian hope, that the mighty would not always
triumph. The archbishop's death had strengthened popular defiance. That elderly couple had made the long
journey to the capital both in homage to Romero and
as an act of opposition. There were scores of thousands
like them in the square.

As we talked, the cathedral began to fill with hundreds
of priests dressed in white. They filled the rows of seats
which had been turned to face out onto the square
behind the open-air altar. The bishops took their places
on the steps around Cardinal Corripio from Mexico,
who was to be celebrant. The coffin was carried out and
laid on the steps before the altar. The Mass began at
around 11 o'clock.

When the sermon began I stood behind the altar and
to the left of the cardinal's chair. In an effort to hear
what was been said, I began to ease my way through the
bishops and priests onto the steps. Suddenly there was
a huge explosion in the far, right-hand corner of the
square. For a split second, there was the feeling of
sitting in a theatre. What was happening in the square

109

was too grotesque, too horrible to be reality. That corner of the square was ablaze and, as shots began to ring out, 100,000 people stampeded. Worst of all was the terrrible crush. Some of the more agile clambered over the high, locked railings in front of the altar. But the children and many poor, over-weight middle-aged women were being crushed against bars.

In the square, people screamed and prayed as they ran clinging to their children. Inevitably families were separated in the panic, and the terror was magnified for those *campesinos* who had to either continue on their own or double back for the elderly and the young. Glimpsing the early seconds of the tragedy, I was terrified. Most distressing of all was the moment of lucidity simultaneously with the first explosion when there was the collective realisation that people were going to be killed. And then people actually were being killed, many of them from heart attacks or trampled underfoot.

The coffin was taken inside. The celebrant's chair was set aside. The gates were opened and a huge mass of humanity tumbled through the gates and clambered up the steps. Anyone who fell (and many did), would be trampled, some to death.

I was swept inside in the first tide of people, and took refuge behind a pillar. A young girl beside me was shivering with terror; she said that her elderly parents had been trampled down as they scrambled into the cathedral. She was sure they were dead. Outside more bombs were going off and shots were being fired. I was told that the attack had come from the Palacio Nacional.

My young companion and I moved to a seat where we were ordered to put our hands over our heads and keep very low. Rumours that people in the cathedral had been shot through the head increased the panic. I was quite certain that I was going to die. Beside me an over-weight pregnant woman in her late thirties went unconscious. Efforts were made to fan her back to life. They failed. The little girl had regained her composure but kept sobbing about her parents. All one could do was hold her hand tightly. Words of consolation or reassurance were quite superfluous. And as I looked at this little girl, old beyond her years, I was reminded that I might never see my own wife and children again.

As in all tragedy, there were instances of black humour. Behind me two ladies sat praying fervently. When they heard me speak, they realised that I was not Salvadorean; and immediately dropped their assault on heaven to reassure me that what I was experiencing was not the real Salvador. I should not mind those out there.

Within minutes, I was sure that armed men would walk up the cathedral steps ten yards away and murder as many people as they had bullets and bombs. "Where are the police and army," I asked with all the indignation of one who had lived in a democracy all his life. "Outside shooting in at us," was the laconic reply from an old man who found it pathetic that anyone could ask such a naive question. This was a lesson in the philosophy of national security.

A chorus of praying and singing could be heard over the sound of bullets and bombs. On the other side of the cathedral, Bishop Casey stood by the door. Afterwards he explained: "People were coming up frightened and terrified. They grabbed you. They embraced you, just to feel the sense of security that things were alright."

Bishop Casey had no Spanish; but that did not seem to hamper communications: "I might have been an El Salvadorean myself. You hugged them, you prayed with them, you prayed for them, they just wanted to feel secure . . . and language did not make any difference. You do not need language at a time like that . . . there was a tremendous at-oneness of the Church with the people because the people who counted are the poor and the oppressed. The rest can look after themselves."

There was no standing on ceremony in the cathedral. It was a time when heroes were made. Bishops and priests stood together with the people. In Latin America, the violence that Sunday was the inevitable outcome of the option for the poor. There was no sense of hierarchy, only Christians facing a common danger. The Church was being attacked; and the main targets of the violence were the ordinary people. Bishop Casey saw twelve bodies at one point lined along the cathedral side wall. "They were the most inoffensive people that the Lord God ever made. Of the twelve I saw together at one stage, eleven of them were women. Most of them in their fifties . . . simple, honest, genuine people to whom Archbishop Romero had been a light in the darkness."

The heat inside the cathedral was overwhelming. Bodies lay on the floor and it was impossible to tell whether they were dead or had just fainted. But one row of elderly women I saw were obviously dead. They had been trampled on, a Red Cross worker told me. About a half an hour after the first explosion, the Red Cross had appeared, and youths wearing that familiar international sign had been rushing out into the square to pick up the injured, the wounded and the dead. I saw one young woman on the floor of the cathedral shot in the leg and in the chest. She received no attention. There was no time and no expertise. Meanwhile, thousands milled around above her.

"I just want to make this point very clearly," Bishop Casey told me in San Salvador, "they were killed by those who started the stampede as clearly and as directly as if they shot them or by whoever planted the bomb. They knew exactly what would happen. And to me it was an act of savagery."

As the shooting began to die down, it was possible to try to reconstruct the events leading to the carnage. Just before the Mass had begun, the Nicaraguan Foreign Minister, Fr Miguel D'Escoto, had been handed a note from his Sandinista security men who had travelled with that government's cabinet to the funeral. It read that there were snipers positioned on the roofs around and that an attack was feared. But it was decided to go ahead with the funeral service. Then as the cardinal began to speak, the Popular Organisations had marched peacefully into the square behind the red banners which I saw being prepared a block away. They marched along the side of the square past the Palacio Nacional and a wreath was passed over the railings and placed beside the coffin.

Shortly after that the first bomb exploded. According to eye-witnesses, it was thrown from the Palacio Nacional at a section of the Popular Organisations. That incident gave rise to the panic, the stampede, and a pitched battle. Youths had come to the square armed, and they returned fire immediately. Cars were overturned and set on fire to provide a smokescreen for the fleeing congregation. Thousands had found refuge in the cathedral itself. However, the majority had scattered into the sidestreets. They were led in files by armed youths who went ahead of the people and fired shots into the air to signal that the way was clear of snipers.

Back in the square, youths had taken up firing positions behind the low cathedral wall. Most of their attention was turned on the Palacio Nacional from where it was claimed that the first bomb had been thrown, followed by rifle and automatic fire. There was little doubt in the cathedral that morning where the violence had begun. The bomb had been thrown from the Palacio, and snipers had been seen on the second floor.

At about half-past one, it was decided that bishops and religious would line up on either side of the laity and walk in file, hands above head, into the now deserted streets as protection, for the snipers were still in the Palacio Nacional. That idea was abandoned when members of the Popular Organisations counselled that it was relatively safe for people to leave alone. Then the long procession began. Nuns walked out through the side door hands held high, a humiliating act of surrender undertaken to placate the trigger-happy snipers. Inside the cathedral, a small group of bishops and clergy gathered around the crypt where Archbishop Romero was to be buried. The funeral service was not hurried. The funeral service was not just for the murdered archbishop; about fifty had been killed that day and five hundred had been taken to hospital. Even those horrifying statistics did not reflect the true extent of the day's violence. Many country people refused to go to hospital. They wanted to get out of the capital as quickly as possible.

But, as I left the cathedral with my hands above my head, I was not aware of the full extent of the violence. I walked down sidestreets not quite knowing where I was going. The thought kept going through my mind that perhaps a sniper would fire. In the cathedral square, I saw hundreds of abandoned umbrellas, hats and piles of shoes. People had literally taken to their heels. As I walked, I remembered the wounded lying on the floor of the cathedral, alone and twisting in agony; and the dead, those ordinary, simple campesino women, with the final expression of horror, terror and agony felt at the moment of the first bomb recorded on their still faces.

There were no shots. There was no gunman waiting in a doorway. But people were now at their doors peering out at the stream of people walking away from the cathedral at an undignified pace as if by remote control. I made my way back to the house where we had left the car. It was not so much a house as a tenement where each room housed an extended family. There, I became conscious of my shocked condition. I tried to phone Ireland, but all the lines were down. And people began to give me tea, coke and other drinks. They did not consider what had just happened anything unusual. It was normal for El Salvador. Is that possible? One final bid to get through to Dublin without success.

As I was on the phone, a beautiful little girl came over to me with a crumpled piece of paper. "That's our Monsenor," she said showing me a picture of Archbishop Romero which she had carefully torn from a magazine. "Did you know him?" I asked. "Of course," she said, "he was in our local church.""Did you understand what he said?" "Not all," she gestured with her hand. "But did you speak to him?" "Certainly," she said, "the Monseñor speaks with everyone."At that, she folded her treasured piece of paper carefully and walked away.

114

Within a few hours, our small group had begun to reassemble. We related what had happened to each other in the cathedral, and then it was off to the bus terminal where a check was being made to see if everyone from Gotera—where the Franciscans work—had made it back to the bus. There I met one youth who claimed he had been pistol-whipped by the guardia. Everywhere there were people, country people of all ages, walking around without shoes. They had been left behind in the plaza. There were frantic attempts to contact parents, find lost brothers and sisters, or just get on a bus to take them home out of the capital. There was a terrible feeling of gloom and foreboding.

What was most horrifying to the outsider was the sense of normalcy. People expected such violence. They had grown used to it. It was part of their daily lives. Many had run the gauntlet to come to the capital in the first place. They would be marked out as "Romero lovers" in their own isolated villages by members of ORDEN. But they were prepared to stand up and be counted.

Meanwhile, the propaganda battle had begun to capture world headlines. A pitched battle had taken place in the main square of the Salvadorean capital under the spotlight of the international media. How could such a thing happen in a country where the junta was in charge and in control? At four thirty in the evening, the junta issued a statement which claimed that the left were responsible for the bombing and shooting. The attack was planned, according to the statement, in order to steal the body of Romero. The junta also claimed that the popular organisations had kept the bishops and clergy prisoners in the cathedral. Finally the statement added that the security forces had not been in the area. They had been confined to barracks.

In the national seminary, Mgr Urioste was trying to get a meeting together of visiting bishops and representatives of other churches. He wanted to set out the Church's account of the day's events.

I had gone to the convent where Bishop Casey was

staying. He had been anxious to go to the various hospitals to visit and comfort the injured and wounded. He spoke to me for about half an hour about the events of that morning. He described the "savagery" he had seen of "poor, ordinary, timid, hopeful people" being driven by the first bomb into a murderous stampede. At the time, he was not clear who was responsible. He saw the bomb explode in the far right corner of the square near the Palacio Nacional. And then an avalanche of people began to come through the cathedral doors. He was trying to calm people down. They were coming up the steps, frightened and terrified: "they grabbed you, they held you, they embraced you just to feel that sense of security just to feel that things were all right. And that's all I did, I just stood there at the door and allowed people to get whatever security and sympathy they sought from me. I helped people in. Language didn't make any difference. You don't need language in a situation like that."

In fact, the door was the most dangerous place to be at that time as the bombs exploded outside and people crashed through the door to safety. It was a source of some concern to one Franciscan who was looking after Bishop Casey that he stood head and shoulders over most Salvadoreans and was a prime target in his red soutane.

Within hours of the events in the cathedral plaza, about thirty bishops, religious and theologians settled down in the national seminary with Monsenor Urioste, vicar general of San Salvador, to try to reconstruct what had actually happened that morning. The junta statement was already on the international wire services. Some of those present were among the most important clergy and intellectuals in Latin America; there was Bishop Luis Bambarén of Peru, Archbishop Marcos McGrath of Panamá, and the theologian Gustavo Gutierrez. At one point, a number of representatives from the popular movements arrived to give their account of the day's events.

One opposition leader was the "notorious" Juan Chacón—the most wanted man in the country—who had been reported two days previously as being dead. The American Ambassador, Mr. White, went so far as to issue a public statement regretting his death. But Chacón was alive and well.

The bishops, including Dr Casey and other visitors, listened to the opposition leaders and there was some discussion. Finally, Bishop James O'Brien of Westminster made a decisive intervention setting out in a very logical way a terse statement outlining what had happened in contradiction to some of the claims made by the junta. One Salvadorean had drawn up a more philosophical document, an extraordinary feat of industry in such a short time. But the meeting opted for the more direct style of the English bishop, and produced a letter which all present signed. This letter referred to the junta's statement and added that "there are not only grave falsehoods in the outlining of events, but also in their interpretation, that could result in grave errors and confusion." The bishops' letter went on to state that "at no time did anyone try to steal the body of Monseñor Romero. On the contrary, all the people and groups without exception, conducted themselves with great respect and devotion towards the remains." And it added, the *Coordinadora Revolucionaria de Masas,* or popular movements, entered the square "peacefully, respectfully and in an orderly fashion," and their leaders brought a wreath to the remains.

It was also untrue, the letter said, that the popular movements made prisoners of anyone or obliged bishops to remain inside the cathedral. If the hierarchy and religious had stayed until the violence had ceased, it was because of their Christian duty to keep the terrorised people company in the sacred precincts.

What the bishops saw from the steps and what they heard in the streets was as follows: A sudden explosion was heard made by a large bomb which various witnesses were sure they had seen being thrown from the *Palacio Nacional;* then machinegun fire and shots were heard. A number of priests present were sure they came from the second floor of the same building; the security forces could be seen in the streets of the capital from early morning and in the approaches to the city. Finally the letter stated that the bishops were convinced that the popular organisations had undertaken a number of actions consisting mainly of burning cars, supposedly to ensure that people could flee.

The letter concluded by stating that the bishops had come to honour the life and death of Monseñor Romero and could give testimony to the truth of his words when he denounced unrelentingly the repression of the Salvadorean people. The bishops had felt that day, more than ever before, the solidarity and continuity with his prophetic mission. They wanted to repeat Romero's last words in which he implored and ordered that the military should stop the repression. The letter was a blunt rejection of the junta's statement.

Greater credibility ought to be attached to this letter from the visiting bishops. The bishops were present in the cathedral. The government was not. At best, the junta had held the ring while the fighting went on.

Later that evening Monsenor Urioste and Bishop O'Brien went to visit the papal nuncio who had attended the funeral. In fact, he had the unpleasant experience in the cathedral of having one of the priests on hunger strike accuse him in a loud voice of being an enemy of the people.[8] He agreed with his visitors that Cardinal Corripio's undelivered sermon should be published in full in the national press as an advertisement. It would not be carried by the government-controlled media otherwise.[9] At the nunciature it was also agreed that the Salvadorean National Episcopal Conference should issue a statement supporting the letter from the visiting bishops.[10]

At this point it was vital that the Salvadorean Church should demonstrate unity. The papal nuncio was in a position to take a strong stand. But things went very wrong for the local church. From Mexico the Salvadorean press carried a report that Cardinal Corripio had

118

spoken of confusion in El Salvador and that he refused to lay blame for the killings during the funeral.[11]

When the Salvadorean bishops met on Wednesday, three days after the funeral, they issued a statement which mentioned the arrival in the square of the *Coordinadora Marxista de Masas*. In fact, the usual title, the *Revolutionary Coordinators of the Masses,* carried no mention of Marx; but the Marxist term had been used in the junta's statement. The Salvadorean bishops spoke of armed youths being present in the cathedral while the visiting bishops were isolated from what was going on outside. And they blamed those same young men as being partly responsible for the violence which held sway in the countryside.

Although the statement was signed by all the bishops of Salvador, its credibility was weakened considerably by the fact that only one of them, Bishop Rivera Damas, was present at the funeral.

Meanwhile, the government lost no time in pressing home their claim that the violence was started by the popular organisations. A press conference was held on March 31, the day after the tragic events of the Plaza Barrios. All five members of the junta were present. They displayed pictures of armed youths firing from around the cathedral. José Napoleon Duarte, a Christian Democrat, related how Fr Miguel d'Escoto had telephoned him from the cathedral requesting that he withdraw the tanks from around the square. He replied that all the soldiers were confined to barracks by order of the junta. Duarte claimed he agreed to call the Red Cross. The Nicaraguan Foreign Minister had in fact, according to Duarte, telephoned three times. Such panic simply illustrated the degree of confusion within the cathedral, according to the junta. All five members blamed the popular organisations for the violence, and Dr. Ramon Avalos Navarrete claimed that the plans for the disruption of the service had been announced on Moscow radio.[12]

But the confusion over what had happened that Sunday was most pronounced in the countryside where radio and television and newspapers bombarded the campesinos. Few had heard of the visiting bishops' letter. That was only something that could be passed on by word of mouth. There were 100,000 in the square for the Romero funeral, many of whom came from the countryside. These saw what had happened and would relate what they had witnessed. The version of the ordinary person in the square was slightly different to what the junta had been saying. But even if people had not actually heard from an eye-witness what had happened, they treated the government statements with a considerable degree of scepticism. The visiting bishops' account of what had occurred fast became the standard version of the events.

On April 7, Archbishop John Quinn of San Francisco issued a long account of his experience in the cathedral that Sunday which upheld the points made in the letter of the visiting bishops. He said that while official reports spoke of a "slight disturbance" during the Mass and blamed the left,

> "the fact, however, is that the leftist elements, which we all saw clearly from the altar where I was standing, were peaceful. The fact is that the first bomb was thrown at them. Are we to believe that they threw the bomb at themselves? The fact is that, having put a wreath on the casket, they would not be likely then to disrupt the funeral. The fact is that the oligarchy and the government seemed to be entirely absent from the funeral. Their presence, it would seem, would be a major reason for leftists to create a disruption, and this reason was lacking. A sharpshooter was seen standing on top of one of the government buildings in the square. Security troops were spotted at various points in the city that morning."[13]

Archbishop Quinn, who attended as President of the National Conference of Catholic Bishops, had a different view of the day's events than either the junta or the American ambassador, Mr. White, who had issued a statement also blaming leftist elements.

120

Although the junta claimed that the security forces had been withdrawn to barracks, there were troops guarding the Palacio Nacional. It was from that building that the first bomb was thrown and the firing commenced. Quite a number of people I spoke to, who had been outside the cathedral, were eye-witnesses to that assault. One seminarian related how he saw bombs being thrown from the second floor.

There is a theory that the violence began as a simple attack on the popular organisations which escalated into a fullscale battle in which ordinary Salvadoreans died. There was a flashpoint in one corner of the square. The marchers were attacked when a bomb was thrown from the *palacio*. They had come prepared and fire was returned. The innocent got caught in the crossfire or were trampled to death.

The idea of a simple accidental encounter leading to widespread violence is a theory which is difficult to sustain. Bombs cannot be manufactured instantaneously. It is also rather unlikely that the popular organisations provoked the confrontation. The possibility of an extreme leftwing group resorting to high machiavellianism cannot be ruled out. But no ecclesiastical source in San Salvador would accept that point of view. The junta statement about the left trying to steal the body of Romero was quite absurd as the visiting bishops testified.

After making extensive inquiries, I find it most probable that the attack was quite deliberately aimed at both the popular organisations and their supporters—that is, anyone who was in the square or in the cathedral that day. A decision had obviously been taken by a rightwing group to attack the funeral. The plans were laid with great care and bombs were planted in different parts of the square. The Palacio Nacional was used as a centre for the attack. The junta never satisfactorily explained why firing had taken place from the most tightly guarded building in the capital. Those who were firing from the palacio were either security force personnel or individuals who were doing so with the knowledge of the guard.

121

In the past, the Palacio Nacional had been used as a vantage point to shoot at demonstrators assembling in the square below. The cathedral had been attacked and people shot on the steps. History repeated itself that Sunday, March 30, 1980. There is nothing staggeringly unusual about such a happening in Central America where demonstrations are attacked without scruple. The funeral of the archbishop offered an unparalleled opportunity to demonstrate the strength of the right and their capacity to follow up on their terror tactics. Those who continued to listen to Archbishop Romero's teachings, broadcast by his many clerical and lay disciples, had also to be instructed in the doctrine of national security. Moreover, the Salvadorean right had a chance to teach the entire church of Latin America a costly lesson—a demonstration of authoritarian logic.

Proaño, Bambarén, Mendez Arceo, Gutierrez read like a Who's Who of Latin American liberation theology. They were all in the cathedral that Sunday along with many others who are well-known for their support of the "preferential option for the poor". In many ways, they had both helped to build Romero's self confidence in his mission and had, in turn, learned from him. The terror tactics in the Plaza Barrios were not just designed to intimidate the Salvadoreans, but were to be a lesson to that entire section of the Church which took the Romero line, or more precisely, the supporters of Medellín, of Paul VI's *On the Development of Peoples,* and of the teaching of John Paul II. The doctrine of geopolitics knows no national boundaries. Neither, of course, does the legacy of Romero. His words, his example, his martyrdom pose a much more serious challenge to the philosophy of national security than the violent rhetoric or actions of any guerrilla group.

Chapter Five

BASTA YA!

Monseñor has left this land.
(He was) crushed by that beast.
"The prophets go to heaven,"
sang a poet; and that is the hope
that he wins in heaven with his blood,
so opening the history of the new men.

His ideal was freedom,
everyone living in community.
He followed the footsteps of Christ,
always ready to shoulder the cross.
Today his light shines as brightly
as a hot sun in El Salvador.

All the forces can carry on;
we can cope with all tribulations.
Our bishop is calling on us
to fight on; we have to move.
A great martyr has shed his blood,
which is the hope of El Salvador.

We've had enough, we've had enough,
we've had enough of death and falsehood.
We've had enough, we've had enough
is the cry of El Salvador.

From the poem, *Basta Ya (Enough)*

Perhaps Archbishop Romero, above everybody else,
would have been most surprised that his name should
have caught the imagination of the entire Catholic
world. He had lived most of his life in comparative

obscurity ministering in El Salvador, the smallest of the national security states in Latin America. His was a minority voice among his national episcopal colleagues. Yet when he received an honorary doctorate at Louvain on February 2, 1980, it was clear that many had begun to recognise that they were listening to a prophetic voice. The message of the fearlessly delivered sermons in the cathedral of San Salvador each Sunday had belatedly begun to find an international audience.

That was not only because of the courageous championing of human rights in a country where the poor are regarded as drudges, but because he had touched a universal Christian chord; he had stripped the message of the Gospel down to its very essence. He had established a series of priorities which were as personally demanding as they were central to the basic Christian message. The result was that his funeral became an occasion of pilgrimage for the entire Catholic Church.

It was the least that people could do, as Bishop Eamon Casey of Galway said on his arrival in San Salvador. To be present to show solidarity with a persecuted and beleaguered Christian people on the occasion when over 100,000 people thronged the square in front of the cathedral to attend the funeral in defiance of those who had murdered the Archbishop presented its own imperative: the Christian had no alternative but to be there.

Although the murder of the archbishop deprived a local church of a powerful and fearless leader, the legacy of Romero may prove a greater threat to those who oppose basic Christian values than the archbishop in his lifetime. That single bullet created a Christian martyr. The blood of martyrs has always been the source of inspiration for a religious revival.

Within days of the Archbishop's murder, his picture was to be found everywhere in El Salvador. Tattered, dog-eared photographs torn from magazines were placed in the homes of the poor. Those who could afford it bought his photo for about 30p a time. In a country where both press and the broadcasting media are strictly controlled, his message has been broadcast by word of mouth throughout the land. Graffiti proclaim his martyrdom from mud walls. Banners with messages of defiance have been hung on railings taunting the authorities.

There is a curious parallel between the death of the Nicaraguan journalist, Pedro Joaquin Chamorro—one of the main opponents of Somoza—and that of Archbishop Romero[1]. Both were fearless defenders of human rights, and died in similar circumstances. In the case of the former, his murder acted as an inspiration to opposition groups in Nicaragua and brought a wave of international anti-Somoza revulsion in the wake of the killing. However, the Romero case is quite different at another level. He was not a journalist but an archbishop; and his witness was an essentially Christian one.

No doubt there are those who will try to use the Romero name for crudely political purposes. One peasant I met, proudly showed me his picture of the archbishop. On the back was a political message from one of the popular organisations, the possessioin of which could have resulted in his death irrespective of the fact that he was illiterate.

The Romero legacy will continue to be interpreted by different people in different ways. Quite tragically, for many of his fellow bishops in Salvador, his memory will remain tainted by the highly personalised perceptions of men who believe that he "divided the church," destroyed episcopal and clerical unity, and fomented class hatred and civil disorder by encouraging popular opposition forces in the country. All such charges are quite groundless. But that does not prevent them from being repeatedly made by men who ought to know better.

The Jesuit theologian, Jon Sobrino, who gave me a long interview two days before the funeral, said that such charges were nothing new. The charge of subverting the people was made against Jesus of Nazareth, he said. "It's simply false."

Did Romero divide the hierarchy then? Answering in

125

a general way, Fr Sobrino said that while he did not want to pass any judgement on people, and certainly not on their conscience which only God knew; it was true, objectively speaking, "there are many bishops who need conversion."[2]

Romero stood in the tradition of Bartolomé de las Casas who was known as the protector of the Indians. He spoke for the poor. In that sense, the murdered archbishop followed the "preferential option" mooted at Puebla. That was very much in keeping with the central teaching of the Church. The conservative stance of the majority of Salvadorean bishops, who either refused or were unable, to apply the central social message of Paul VI's encyclical, *On the Development of Peoples,* had cut themselves off from the mainstream of Catholic thought. It was not Romero who was out of step. His sternest critics were, and this had the most tragic consequences for the Salvadorean church.

In fact, Romero revivified the Church in his country, despite the strong antagonisms to him in the ranks of the powerful and the wealthy, he managed to attract not just the poor but many middle and upper class people away from the path of religious indifference. It was that ability to confirm people in their faith which Jon Sobrino considers to be of most importance in the witness of Oscar Romero.

The second important aspect of the archbishop's life was his total commitment to the defence of the poor. And that was a point which emerged most convincingly in his address at Louvain when he told his distinguished audience that "for us, the world which the Church should serve, is the world of the poor." He added:

> "It is, then, a simple fact that our Church has been persecuted for the past three years. But it is most important to observe why it has been persecuted. They have not attacked just any priest or institution. But they have attacked that very part of the Church which has sided with the poor and come out in their defence. And yet again do we find the key to understanding the persecution of the Church: the POOR."[3]

Fr Sobrino indicated what exactly that meant. Romero denounced sin in its very concrete reality. He denounced the politics of the national security state. He denounced the capitalistic system, "which for Salvadoreans is a source of misery and death." He denounced the repression of military men and the repressive forces. He denounced the "genocide, and I'm saying this very consciously," Fr Sobrino added; "I know it's a very strong word, but this is what is happening in the last two months in this country."[4]

An example of just how strongly Archbishop Romero spoke out against sin in society can also be found in the Louvain address:

> "The real persecution has been directed at poor people, who are today the Body of Christ in history. They are the crucified people, like Jesus, the persecuted people like the Servent of Yahweh. It is they who complete in their body the passion of Christ. . . "[5]

Now what exactly did sin mean for the murdered archbishop:

> "We know that death of man is an offence to God. We know that sin is truly mortal but not only because of the internal death of the person who commits it, but because of the real and objective death which it produces. We recall that profound truth of our Christian religion: sin is that which killed the Son of God and sin continues to be that which kills the the children of God. . . . . It is not out of pure routine that we repeat once more the existence of the structures of sin in our country. They are sinful because they produce the fruits of sin: the death of Salvadoreans, be it the rapid death resulting from repression or the slow — but nonetheless real — of structural oppression. Because of that we have denounced the idolatory of wealth, of absolute private property in the capitalist system, and of political power in national security regimes in whose name the insecurity of the individual is institutionalised."

It is clear that sin had a very concrete reality for Archbishop Romero, which had a social as well as an individual dimension. But he also took this question a stage further in his teaching. Sin had to be denounced. But the Good News had also to be proclaimed. But not *just* proclaimed. The Christian social reality had to be constructed. That was where the real danger of Romero's teaching lay for the military and the oligarchy.

But perhaps the archbishop's most original contribution lay in Romero's concept of his episcopal office as *service*. He derived his strength from the Word of God and the People of God whom he visited in their villages and slums not simply as a task of his office but as a real pleasure. He had a profound respect for the ordinary people. He admired their courage and their faith and he derived inspiration from them. Moreover, he listened to what they had to say. There was real dialogue. Romero had a strongly collegial spirit. As a consequence, the People of God articulated views which he as archbishop was obliged to listen to most attentively.

Such a theology had the most profound consequences for his theology of the ministry. One example of his capacity for dialogue was that he circularised his people before leaving for Puebla in Mexico to attend the conference of Latin American bishops. He wanted to find out what *they* felt he ought to raise for discussion. Moreover, his use of power as leader of the Salvadorean Church was exemplary. Usually the Church dialogues with the civil powers on behalf of the people. The structure is pyramidical. But in Romero's case the Church was the community of the People of God. The power of that Church was with the people. The power of the Church was what the people already had or should have. As a result, the Church in Salvador has somewhat paradoxically developed great social power despite the fact that it shunned an alliance with the civil authorities.

Romero put that point very clearly:

"It is the role of the Church to gather into itself all that is human in the people's cause and struggle, above all in the cause of the poor. The Church identifies with the poor when they demand their legitimate rights. In our country, the right they are demanding is hardly more than the right to survive, to escape from poverty . . . faith which is lived out in isolation from life is not true faith."

Such identification with the poor led to persecution. Throughout Latin America some thirty six priests have been killed violently, and of these six died in guerrilla fighting. Over two hundred and forty have been expelled from various countries. About one hundred were expelled from Chile in 1973 after the overthrow of Allende. In Venezuela seven were asked by the local hierarchy not to return. In Guatemala foreign priests must leave the country every three months largely at the insistence of the conservative archbishop, Cardinal Casariego. By ensuring that missionary priests must leave the country regularly, he has the power to determine what priests should be allowed stay.

Many more examples could be cited of the worsening human rights situation in Latin America, and of the divisions within the Church. But the polarisation between conservative and, for want of a better word, progressive clergy must be understood in the light of the Romero experience in El Salvador. The charge was constantly laid in the past that clergy were very much on the side of the rich. If that was ever the case, it certainly is not so now. There has been a shift in recent times which has caught the traditional oligarchies off guard. The Catholic Church is now seen as something of a Trojan horse in the national security states.

It is only when one understands the rank poverty of the majority of Salvadoreans that it is possible to comprehend the basic selfishness of the rich on the one hand, and the desperation of the poor on the other. The social problems are vast; the country is reminiscent of Victorian Britain where the majority lived their lives in

Statistics of repression against the Church 1964–1978

	Menaces Calumnies	Attacks Arrests Imprisonment	Torture	Murder	Kidnappings	Expulsion Exile
Total	245	788	71	69	21	279
Bishops	53	21	—	1	1*	1
Priests	117	485	46	36**	5	245***
Religious	2	27	7	—	2	26
Lay persons	9	255	18	31	13	7
Groups	64	—	—	—	—	—

* Kidnapping of Cardinal Casariego (Guatemala), known for his ultra-conservative opinions; an unexplained event.
** Of these, six died in guerilla fighting; three more have been killed in El Salvador.
*** About 100 priests were expelled from Chile in 1973; 7 in Venezuela were asked by the local hierarchies not to return.

hopelessness and squalor. Radical changes are demanded by the Gospel in such an economic structure but their impact would be so great that the closed world of the rich would be shattered. They would not be impoverished by any means. But their antiquated world order of privilege would pass away. That possibility is too horrible for them to comprehend. Hence the tacit acceptance of rightwing violence which runs counter to the basic Christian philosophy they purport to hold so strongly. That phenomenon of fear feeding on greed is common to many Latin American countries. Salvador is no exception.

Pax Americana

There is little evidence to suggest that the US State Department is actually aware of what constitutes the popular organisations. Therefore, the movements which enjoy the active support of the overwhelming majority of the Salvadorean people are depicted as being leftwing. That, of course, is a serious analytical mistake. There is a very basic campaign being waged in Salvador to secure fundamental human rights which transcends the purely political realm.

Yet the Washington view remains unchanged; one official US source summarised the situation: "Extremists of both left and right are attempting to bring down the government. Rightist groups opposed to all reforms are engaging in indiscriminate asassinations and hope to instigate a reactionary countercoup. Leftist cadres see power slipping from their grasp and are provoking confrontations in hope of stimulating a violent revolution."

In order to proceed with the reforms in the face of special interests, the Salvadorean government has, according to Washington, been forced to "institute a limited state of siege, suspending temporarily certain constitutional guarantees." However, US policy has welcomed and supported the government's efforts believing that the October 15 programme offered the best chance for evolutionary reform, political liberalization, and respect for human rights in El Salvador.

This US policy has bestowed international respectability on the junta. Further, the US has provided economic assistance of about $50m for the 1980 financial year to aid agrarian and other reform programmes. And finally, military assistance of $5.7 million in foreign sales credits has enabled the Salvadorean armed forces "to purchase communication and transportation equipment, which will help them protect implementation of the reform program against violence from both right and left."[6]

But it is quite inadequate to explain political violence in Salvador in purely national terms. It is impossible, in fact, to discuss domestic political affairs of Latin American countries without reference to the role of the United States. It probably was no coincidence that Archbishop Romero was murdered a short time after he had written to President Carter requesting the halting of arms shipments to his country. The "stability" of the national security state generally, and Salvador in particular, depend very heavily on the munificence of Washington. When Romero made his plea he was really requesting that the American president should cut a life-line to the oligarchy and the military. Although the truth of the assassination will probably never be known, it is probable that that intervention, coupled with his direct appeal to soldiers over the heads of the officer class to stop the repression, precipitated his assassination by an extremist rightwing group.

The American attitude towards the junta in Salvador is of crucial importance:

"It is the view of the United States Government that the reform program of the Revolutionary Junta offers the best possibility of resolving El Salvador's serious and multiple problems. Therefore, we are providing assistance to the Junta. Our objective is to promote ecomomic reform in El Salvador while

132

simultaneously **enlarging** the degree of political liberty. This is a difficult but not, we believe, an ultimately unattainable objective."[7]

That is a policy with which many leading Catholic intellectuals in Salvador profoundly disagree. The entire strategy pre-supposes that the junta possess effective power which they obviously *did not* in the early part of 1980.

In Salvador, there is a certain paranoia about American influence, especially on the left. There, the source of all evil is Washington and the machinations of the CIA. On the extreme right, there is a sense of betrayal. They have seen Nicaragua fall to the Sandinistas. They have seen the U.S. "sell out" over the Panama Canal and they fear that Salvador will be just one more domino to fall in the Central American region to the "wiles of communism".

The truth is that there are many faces to U.S. foreign policy and interests in El Salvador—some of them ugly. But it is too simplistic to let the matter rest there. The history of American colonial involvement in the hemisphere has made it particularly difficult for a liberal president of the U.S. to convince people of his goodwill. People do not require long memories to recall what happened in Chile under Allende or in Guatemala in the mid-1950s.

The provincial of the Jesuits in Central America, Fr Cesar Jerez, is a good example of a liberal Latin American intellectual who can fairly evaluate U.S. policies. In fact, Fr Jerez, who lives in San Salvador, had the benefit of post-graduate studies in Chicago. And when he addressed an audience at Canisius College there, he referred to the recent political experience of his native Guatemala. He explained that he had been greatly impressed by his professors in Chicago who had led him to study Paolo Friere's *conscientizacion* and its meaning for the building up of real democracy in central American countries. But when he returned to Guatemala in 1972 there was no democracy.

"On the other hand, if you are familiar with the history of this tiny central American "banana" or "coffee" republic as your own history books called it, you will know that in 1953 there *was* democracy in Guatemala. As your former President, Dwight D. Eisenhower, has acknowledged in his memoirs, and I do not say "confessed" because there is no repentance in the acknowledgement, 1954 was the year in which the CIA helped our own conservative forces in Guatemala to overthrow the democratically elected regime of President Jacobo Arbenz. Why did this terrible thing happen? It happened because the Arbenz regime was stigmatized as communist precisely when the cold war mentality was at its peak, when Joe McCarthy destroyed careers and assassinated characters in your own country on the flimsy grounds that they were 'soft on Communism'."[8]

Jerez went on to point out that Arbenz had merely intended to modernise the country, turning it from a semi-feudal into a full-fledged capitalist society independent of the United States. He intended to create a new class of small farmers. In other words, he was a model exponent of Walt Rostow's *Stages of Growth*. The only problem, according to Fr Jerez, was the fact that he "wanted to become independent of the U.S. while being geopolitically located in its backyard" during the cold war. But that policy ran counter to the State Department and the United Fruit Company's plans for Guatemala.[9]

So, paradoxically, "democracy" had to be defended against the aspirations of Guatemalan democracy. And Fr Jerez contrasted the absolute right to private property, as conceived by the Bill of Rights and the Declaration of Independence, "with the highly unreasonable and even murderous right to a free hand in the consolidation of transnational corporations. The attitude of Anaconda and of Richard Nixon, of the CIA and of the Pentagon towards Allende's nationalistic Second Declaration of Independence in 1971 was similar to the

134

attitude of the United Fruit Company and John Foster Dulles towards the second Guatemalan Declaration of Independence in 1952."[10]

Fr Jerez had touched on themes that should shed new light on the study of Salvador. It is unfortunately true that the picture of the ugly American predominates in Central America. This prominent Jesuit pointed to the double standard which, he argued, obtained in the formulation of U.S. policies. There was one code for domestic politics and quite another for countries within the U.S. sphere of influence. Unfortunately, it is not possible to wipe the slate of history clean and start afresh. And the State Department is not the sole arbiter of American presence in Salvador. The Pentagon and the CIA are more concerned with military, strategical and geopolitical considerations than with the defence of human rights. Furthermore, there is the role played by the multinational companies who stand to lose so much because of nationalistic economic decisions by Latin American governments. In recent years there have also developed paramilitary rightwing groupings who are determined to save their world from communism, even if there is no significant threat from that quarter, and which are prepared to support and finance groups such as ORDEN and the White Warriors.

There is no way of proving this analysis conclusively other than to say that it is widely believed in Salvador. Moreover, the multinationals are very much independent agents capable of acting with a frightening degree of sovereignty, and with scant respect for the State Department line when it does not suit them. Conversely, the oligarchy are in a position to exert pressure on any administration through the coffee lobby in the United States and through other orthodox economic channels.

Archbishop Romero was very much aware of these factors, and for that reason he made his direct appeal to President Carter to stop the supply of arms to the military who were directly involved in repression, irrespective of the protestations of innocence by the junta. There are parallel governments in Salvador. The official civilian military junta is powerless while the real force is an amorphous group of faceless tyrants determined to use the very ultimate in terror tactics to keep society as it has been for decades—safely in the hands of the oligarchy.

For that reason Romero pleaded for his followers in one of his most famous sermons:

"If anytime they stop the radio, ban the papers, deny us the possibility of speaking, kill all the priests and the bishops too; and they leave you a pueblo without priests, everyone of you must be a microphone of God—everyone of you must be a messenger, a prophet; the church will always exist in the world for as long as there remains one baptised person and that last baptised person who remains in the world, is he who has the responsibility before the entire world to maintain the flag of Our Lord's truth and Divine Justice flying high."

Romero was murdered along with six of his priests and thousands of ordinary people over the past three years. Yet despite the martyrdom of so many, the slaughter has continued unchecked.

The wounded hope

Unfortunately, this account must end with Salvador in agony. How better to describe that "crucifixion" than in the words of one of the country's foremost poets, Francisco Andrés Escobar. In June, 1977 the security forces carried out an intensive operation in Aguilares—the region where the murdered Jesuit, Rutilio Grande, had worked—in an effort to capture campesinos, workers, priests and students accused of "subversion". The outcome was predictably violent. The experience of Aguilares was later to overtake the entire country. Francisco Andrés Escobar called his poem "Martyr People".[11]

PUEBLOMARTIR

I

Yesterday, here, the demons came
dressed in lean green leaf.

Yesterday, here, the bells rang
like a premonition of agony.

Here the moon covered its face
not to see the ritual of the lances.

Here the cock was unable to crow
because the shrapnel struck it dumb.

Here the clear waters darkened
to become torrents of scarlet.

Here Christ suffered on the violated alb,
stole and sanctuary.

Here the rifle gleaned in days
of apostles and of angels.

Here the cane and maize field flourish
watered with the blood of martyrs.

II

Disturbed is the soft passage of the mist,
broken the quiet movement of the worlds,
wrenched out the tears!
Wounded the fragile mirror of the waters,
the pale shell of life!
Wounded the hope!

III

Ah, traveller, do not pass by!
Come into these streets for they walk in trance,
seeking the dead amongst the shadows

and wiping away hope's tears!
Come into these streets,
go through this blood:
the deep "via crucis" of the flesh!
Grief's cathedral of a thousand naves
has suffering painted on its inmost parts.
Come in, traveller,
do not pass by!
and later go to your distant land
and say to the faces, to the winds,
to the bird, to the pine and to the fountains,
to the shade, to the light, to the deserts,
to all that live and hope and love,
that this "pueblo" that until yesterday was Aguilares
is henceforth called PUEBLOMARTIR.

The poem was prompted by the following incident.
Following the murder of Fr Rutilio Grande in March,
1977, the town of Aguilares and the surrounding area
became a centre of particular military attention. Campesinos had occupied farms, and had called the appropriated land after Rutilio, Manuel and Nelson (the
Christian names of those killed in the attack on the
priest's jeep). About two thousand soldiers, aided by
helicopters, took part in an operation to evict the two
hundred peasants. Many people "disappeared" in the
operation. But that manoeuvre was followed by a more
elaborate campaign against the peasant organisations.
   On May 19, 1977, the day after the evictions, a large
force of soldiers surrounded a zone of about five
hundred square kilometres, including the towns of El
Paisnal, Suchitoto, and Tacachico. Thousands of people
were rounded up. Their homes were sacked, looted,
and destroyed. A dusk to dawn curfew was imposed.
And the press and Red Cross were prohibited from
entering the area. As an act of calculated profanity,
military headquarters were set up in Rutilio Grande's
church at Aguilares. There, people were interrogated,
tortured, and imprisoned, while the bodies of dead and

wounded were piled up in the nave. The number of those killed in the Aguilares operation has never been satisfactorily calculated.

Horrifying incidents of repression continue in Salvador. For instance, May 1980, was a particularly violent month. There were military search-and-destroy missions in the areas of El Trifinio and near San Vincente (Amatepec). The state of siege made reporting impossible. But in neighbouring Honduras *El Tiempo* reported that three hundred and twenty people had been killed in a massacre at the Sumpul river, which marks the border between El Salvador and Honduras.

When the two governments denied the newspaper reports, the bishop and priests of the Honduran diocese of Santa Rosa de Copan issued a statement reconstructing the horrifying events of May 14, 1980.

The day before the massacre, there was considerable troop movement on the Honduran side, around Guarita, with forces taking up positions along the banks of the Sumpul. On the Salvadorean side, La Arada was crowded with refugees — mainly old men, women, and young children, fleeing the violence in their areas, and hoping to gain the comparative safety of neighbouring Honduras.

The massacre began at about 7 a.m. At least two helicopters supported the ground forces — soldiers, national guard, and members of the para-military group, ORDEN. The statement from the bishop and clergy described what happened:

> They opened fire on the defenceless people. Women were tortured right up to the final "tiro de gracia." Children at the breast were thrown in the air and used as targets. These were some of the scenes of this criminal massacre. The refugees who wanted to cross the river were turned back into the area of the massacre by the Honduran soldiers. By the middle of the afternoon the genocide ceased, leaving a total of at least six hundred bodies.

The bodies were simply left where they fell, to be

eaten by dogs or to be washed downstream. One fisherman recovered "five little bodies of children" in his nets. The river Sumpul was contaminated as far as Santa Lucia.

A very sinister aspect of the massacre was that it was a combined operation by the security forces of the two neighbouring countries. The statement of the bishop of Santa Rosa de Copan reported that a few days before the massacre senior military officers from Guatemala, El Salvador, and Honduras met secretly at Ocotepeque, on the Guatemalan frontier.[12]

Is there any possible explanation for such an event? The helicopters and the scale of the operation would indicate that it was a lesson in sheer terror. The message to the *pueblo* was unmistakable — there is no place to hide or to find safety outside your own country.

Month by month, such atrocities continue in El Salvador. Yet, despite the repression, for the ordinary people hope though wounded has not been extinguished. The "quiet movement of the worlds" has been broken, tears wrenched out, and the "fragile mirror of the water wounded." Yet the poor and the wretched still have the fortitude, the faith and the hope to sing out in daily defiance:

You are the God of the poor,
a human and a simple God,
the God who sweats in the street,
the God of the withered face.
That's why I speak to you
just like my people speak,
because you are the worker God,
the labouring Christ.

And so sing the *pueblomartir*.

THE CREEPING COUP

As the violence of the "parallel government" against the ordinary Salvadoreans grew in intensity late in 1980, two episodes in particular helped bring home to the outside world yet again the horror of the political repression. These were the murders of the five top opposition leaders, and of four Catholic missionaries.

The first incident occurred when the five men were attending an FDR "shadow cabinet" meeting in the Jesuit school of San José in central San Salvador. Fifteen armed and masked men burst into the room, selected their victims, and took them away at gunpoint. At the time of the attack the school was surrounded by police; although there were eyewitnesses, this allegation was flatly denied by official sources.[1]

The body of Enrique Alvarez Cordova, Secretary General of the FDR, was found a day later outside the capital. He had been shot in the chest, but before that he had been tortured — one of his arms was severed from his body by a machete blow. Cordova was one of the most popular and highly respected political figures in Salvador. Unlike many of his FDR colleagues, he was from a wealthy background. He was a landowner, and his parents were numbered among the "Fourteen Families." He was at the heart of the fight to nationalise and redistribute land, having given his own extensive lands to the peasants. He had served as Minister for Agriculture under the first and second juntas. But when the planned social revolution was frustrated by the militant right, Cordova resigned in protest at the growing violence in the country and the implication of the military in the killings. When the FDR was formed in April, 1980, he became secretary general. His murder on a lonely road outside the capital mirrored the deaths of his four captured colleagues.

Juan Chacon, the articulate twentythree year old

leader of the combined popular organisations, was also murdered. I had met him several times in El Salvador, and I believe he could have risen to the top of the trade union movement in any country.[2] His bullet-ridden body, clenched fist still raised above his body in an act of final defiance, was found along with those of Manuel Franc of the National Democratic Union, Humberto Mendoza of the Popular Liberation Movement, and the Social Democrat, Ernesto Barrera. The secretary of LP 28, Leonocio Pichinte, and three other activists were also kidnapped from the meeting.

The "anti-communist" Brigade of Maximiliano Hernandez Martinez quickly claimed responsibility for the *ajusticiamento,* or pay-off. The name of the group carries its own terror. It will be remembered that General Hernandez was responsible for the massacre of thirty thousand peasants in 1932. The brigade justified the killing of the five politicans on the grounds that they were "materially and intellectually responsible for thousands of assassinations of innocent people who did not want to become communists." Their statement also warned priests "who were in league with terrorist Marxist bands that they would run the same risk (as the murdered men) if they continue to insist in their sermons on poisoning the minds of the youth."[3]

In the second incident three American nuns and a lay missionary, Jean Donovan, who had spent a year studying at University College, Cork, disappeared while returning from the airport at night. All that is known for certain about that journey is its horrible outcome: The women's bodies were found in shallow graves; all had been raped and shot. The evidence points to military being implicated for it is impossible to travel that lonely road from the airport to the capital without encountering checkpoints.[4]

A State Department team was sent from Washington to investigate the killings, and US aid to the junta was suspended. Although there was considerable circumstantial evidence implicating the security forces, the Washington investigators could find no direct evidence of military involvement, and US aid was resumed in December 1980.

Although the killings of the missionaries brought home to Americans and Europeans the horror of the violence in Salvador, there was something horribly normal about the murders. Thousands of ordinary Salvadoreans had suffered the same fate.

The killing of the political leaders symbolised the complete dominance of the radical right. For by then the radical right had infiltrated the administration, merging with the political and military figures until government and "parallel government" were fused. In what Salvadoreans term the "creeping coup", the oligarchy completed its stranglehold on the country.

The fate of Colonel Majano and of Dr Morales Erlich, the two remaining liberal figures in the junta, show the workings of this coup. Being determined to pursue a liberal course within the junta, Colonel Majano had many enemies among the "parallel government." And there had been many attempts to force his resignation. He had been offered ambassadorial posts. His opponents, especially Duarte, had toured the military barracks during the summer to whip up feeling against him. Some of his supporters had been killed in mysterious fashion. And in November, 1980, the intimidation was stepped up: The colonel escaped a bomb attack on his car.[5]

Early in December, 1980, army officers voted overwhelmingly for his removal from the junta, although about four hundred officers refused to take part in the ballot.[6] Claiming that some officers had been ordered to vote against him, Majano saw the military ballot as fraudulent. When he was dismissed from the junta Colonel Majano, who was a close personal friend of the murdered Enrique Alvarez Cordova,[7] commented, "I believe the extreme right has taken control of the government and is holding back the possibility of a specific and political solution to El Salvador's problems."

In an effort to have US aid resumed in Salvador, the government was re-organised in mid-December, 1980.

Duarte was appointed President and the hardliner, Colonel Jaime Gutierrez, who had been conferred with "full powers" by the armed forces, was appointed second-in-command. The junta was disbanded. Gutierrez was supported by Colonel Casanova, head of the National Guard, who had once told the first junta that he was prepared to sacrifice one hundred and fifty thousand people to "restore order" in the country.[8]

The liberal, Dr Morales Erlich, took up the position of Minister of Agriculture. But that did not signify a triumph for moderation. Tolerating the "moderate" was a cosmetic move, designed to ensure the delivery of the $20 million aid package which the killing of the four missionaries had put in jeopardy. By 17 December, 1980, US aid was back on stream. Colonel Majano recognized that the reorganisation of the government was a triumph for the right. Declaring that he would not serve an "illegitimate" government that tolerated military officers who engaged in the activities of right-wing death squads, he went underground. The new government ordered his arrest.

Colonel Majano was probably referring to the failure of the junta to take action when presented with substantial evidence implicating a number of former members of the security forces in the successful plot to murder Archbishop Romero.

This is what had happened: In May, 1980, Colonel Majano ordered a raid on an isolated ranch near Santa Tecla where a group, led by the dismissed head of intelligence, D'Abuisson, was gathered. It was believed that the group was planning a coup. Among the documents captured in the raid was a diary, the property of an aide of D'Abuisson, in which appeared an entry "Operation Starlight." Under this heading appeared a shopping list for an assassination — one telescopic sight, a specific high-powered rifle, a car, and a four-man team who were to fulfil special functions. There were many assassinations in El Salvador in 1980, but few which required the skills of a marksman, and such meticulous preparation. The diary entry was thus a breakthrough in the investigation of Archbishop Romero's murder. D'Abuisson and his associates should have been detained and questioned closely about the murder. Majano had brought the diary to Duarte, indicating that action ought to be taken against those detained after the Santa Tecla raid. But D'Abuisson and the others were sufficiently well connected that, after a few days, they were released without charge. Duarte stood discredited by his inaction. Majano was so incensed that he arranged that copies of the diary entry could be leaked to certain clergy and that "Operation Starlight" could become public knowledge.

Terror continues

The political reshuffle which made Duarte president did nothing to lift the spectre of terror from the country. He was a figurehead without a party, a civilian whose presence in office gave credibility to a regime governing by force of arms. As the army continued to be the agent of rightwing forces in the country, professional morale began to break down among the officers. Some left and joined the Democratic Revolutionary Front (FDR). Others, like Colonel Majano, took longer to commit themselves. Still others, while remaining within the army, did what they could to soften the rigour of repression. Thus the Rector of the Catholic University in San Salvador, Fr Ellacuria, was saved from certain death when a professional army officer warned him of a death squad planning to kill him in two hours. The Jesuit was able to take refuge in the Spanish embassy. The Jesuit community was dispersed, those not directly involved in pastoral work leaving the country. And the house was destroyed by two bombs.

After months of indiscriminate slaughter, which left over twenty thousand dead, popular resistance broke out in a surprisingly strong and well-organised way in January 1981. "What are we to do," one peasant told a priest, "sit in our huts and wait to be killed by the security forces or else fight and die with dignity." On the weekend of 11 January, 1981, the forces of the FDR took the field against the army. The capital was the scene of many gunbattles; but the best-planned guerrilla offensives centred on Santa Ana, the second largest town in the country, in Zacatecoluca, and in San Francisco de Gotera where Irish missionaries have a house across the square from the commando barracks.

The rebels had their most spectacular success in Santa Ana where a captain from the garrison, the same man who had saved the life of Fr Ellacuria, and seventy soldiers joined the guerrillas. They opened the arsenal to the insurgents, who carried away as much as they could for distribution to volunteers. What could not be carried away in time was blown up. A colonel and a number of soldiers were killed as the rebel captain and his supporters fought their way out. With the city easily in the control of the guerrillas, the depleted garrison was easily pinned down for days. Although the Salvadorean airforce had been virtually destroyed by saboteurs, Guatemala provided air support to bomb guerrilla strongholds in Santa Ana.

The January offensive was a real shock to the security forces. Particularly alarming were the defections from their ranks. The most significant of these was the decision of Lt Colonel Ricardo Bruno to join the Farabundo Marti Liberation Front (FMLN). He probably played a substantial role in directing the attack on the commando headquarters in Gotera.

The threat posed by the guerrillas was so strong that President Carter, in one of his last acts before leaving the White House, resumed military aid to the beleaguered "centrist" government. Washington was satisfied that security forces had not been involved in the killings of the three nuns and the lay missionary. And the US ambassador in San Salvador, Mr White, was also concerned about alleged Nicaraguan involvement in the fighting. Within a week the guerrillas melted back to their strongholds to regroup and mobilise for a further assault. Meanwhile in Managua, as the Salvadorean

146

ambassador and his entire staff went over to the FDR, Maryknoll nuns and priests occupied the American embassy in protest at the Carter decision. The European representative of the FDR, Fr Luis de Sebastian SJ, reported confidently that, though the popular organisations could take power by force, that was not what they wanted to do. The guerrilla offensive was simply a demonstration of popular military strength, a necessary measure to get to the conference table with the United States.

The doomsday situation had come about which Archbishop Romero, through his appeals for a peaceful progression to social and political justice, had tried so hard to avoid. While there was nothing inevitable in the Salvadorean process, the triumph of hope seemed probable in January, 1981, if Salvadoreans were left to settle the matter themselves.

In his pastoral, *Political Violence and the Popular Organisations,* Monseñor Romero showed that he was aware of the dilemna of the idealistic Christian in El Salvador. He saw the apparently inexorable drift towards trade union, political and ultimately revolutionary action. Hope must be allowed to triumph. The Christian witness, the courage, the writings and the reputation of Archbishop Romero must be allowed to prevail in his people's struggle for dignity and justice.

BIBLIOGRAPHY

Alves, R. *A Theology of Human Hope*, New York: 1969
Anon. *Los Jesuitas ante el Pueblo Salvadoreno*, Madrid: 1973 *Rutilio Grande*, San Salvador: 1978 *Persecución de la Iglesia en el Salvador*, San Salvador:
Anon. *En memoria de Luis Espinal SJ*, La Paz: 1980

Bataillon Marcel and André Saint Lu, *Las Casas et la défense des indiens* Paris
Boff, Leonardo *Gracia y Liberacion del Hombre*, Madrid: 1978 *Jesucristo el liberador*, Bogota; 1977 *La Vida Mas alla de la muerte*, Bogota: 1977 *Nuestra Resurrección en la muerte*. Bogota: 1978
Bonilla, Victor Daniel, *Servants of God or Masters of Men* (*The Story of a Capuchin Mission in Amazonia*), London: 1971
Bourne, Richard. *Political leaders of Latin America,* London: 1969
Browning, D., *El Salvador, Landscape and Society*, Oxford, 1971
Bruneau, Thomas C., *The Political transformation of the Brazilian Catholic Church*, Cambridge; 1974
Blachman, Moris J. and Hellman, Ronald Gl, (eds.) *Terms of Conflict: Ideology in Latin American Politics*, Philadelphia, 1977

Chevalier, Francois, (trans.) *Land and Society in Colonial Mexico: the great hacienda* Berkely, 1963
Camara, Helder *Race Against Time*, London: 1971 *The Church and Colonialism*, London: 1969
Connor, James L., "El Salvador's Agony and US Policies", *America*, April 26, 1980, pp. 360-362
Colindres, Eduardo, *Fundamentos Economicos de la Burguesia Salvadorena*, San Salvador: 1977
Costello, Gerald M., *Mission to Latin America*, New York: 1979

de Broucker, Jose *Dom Helder Camara: The Conversions of a bishop*, London: 1977
de Dadt, Emanuel and Williams, Gavin, eds., *Sociology and Development*, London: 1974
Dorr, Donal "Third World Theology: Sao Paulo Conference," *Doctrine and Life,* May 1980 pp. 215-227

Ellacuría, Ignacio, *Freedom made Flesh*, New York, 1976

Finer, S. E., *The Man on Horseback*, London: 1962
Flanagan, Padraig *A New Missionary Era: Knock Missionary Union Congress, 1979* Dublin, 1979

Galeano, Eduardo. *Guatemala: Occupied Country*: New York: 1969 trans.

Gerassi, John ed., *Camilo Torres Revolutionary Priest, His complete writings and Messages*; London: 1973; *The Great Fear in Latin America*, New York: 1967

Galilea, Segundo. *Los Pobres nos Evangelizan?* Bogota: 1977

Gallet, Paul *Freedom to Starve*, London: 1970 trans.

Gutierrez, Gustavo *A Theology of Liberation*, New York: 1973

Guillermoprieto, Alma "Rich man poor man," *Guardian*, January 26, 1979

Green, David *The containment of Latin America* Chicago, 1971

Hanke, Lewis, *South America: modern Latin America, continent in Ferment* (2 vols.) New York: 1967

Huntington, S.P., *Political Order in Changing Societies*, New Haven, 1976

Keogh, Dermot "After Romero: United Church, Divided Hierarchy," *Doctrine and Life*, June/July, 1980 pp. 284-291

Lindqvist, Sven *The Shadow: Latin America faces the seventies.* London: 1972 (trans.)

Mariscal, Nicolás, "Militares y reformismo en el Salvador," *ECA*, January-February, 1978 no. 351/352 pp. 9-27

Medawar, Charles, *Insult or Injury.* London: 1979

Mereu, Italo. *Storia dell'Intolleranza in Europa.* Milano: 1979

Melville, Thomas and Majorie, *Guatemala—another Vietnam.* London 1971

Montes, Segundo, *El Compadrazgo.* San Salvador: 1979

Mörner, Magnus *Race Mixture in the History of Latin America*, New York, 1967

MacCarthy, Gerald, "What really happened at Puebla," *The Month*, March 1979 pp. 77-79, 98

McEoin, Gary and Riley, Viveta, "Background to Archbiship Romero's Assassination," *Doctrine and Life,* May 1980 pp. 206-210

Niedergang, Marcel. *The Twenty Latin Americas*, 2 vols. London 1971 trans.

Nichols, Peter "Archbishop Romero: lone voice against tyranny," *Spectator*, March 7, 1979

O'Carroll, Michael *Poland and John Paul 11.* Dublin: 1979

Plant, Roger "Washington's new package: repression and reform—sacrifice of an archbishop," *New Statesman,"* March 28, 1980 p.473.

Proaño, Leonidas E., *Concientización evangelización Politica.* Salamanca: 1975

Perlmutter, A., *The Military and Politics in Modern Times*. New Haven, 1977

Retrato de Camilo Torres, Barcelona, 1968
Romero, Oscar A., Rivera Damas, Arturo, Ellacuría, Ignacio, Sobrino, Jon, and Campos, Tomas R., *Iglesia de los Pobres y Organizaciones Populares*. San Salvador, 1979

Schneider, Ronald M. and Kingsbury, Robert C., *An Atlas of Latin American Affairs*, London: 1966
Segundo, J.L., *A Theology for Artisans of a New Humanity*, 5 vols. New York: 1973-1974; *The Liberation of Theology*, Dublin, 1977
Sobrino, Jon, *Christology at the Crossroads*, London; 1978 trans.
Skidmore, Thomas E., *Politics in Brazil 1930-1964, An experiment in Democracy*. Oxford, 1960
Sweeney, John "Praying the Passion in Latin America Today," *Scripture in Church*, Lent and Easter, 1980, No 38 pp. 414-426

Tannenbaum, Frank, *Ten Keys to Latin America*, New York, 1962; *The Future of Democracy in Latin America*, New York, 1964
Torres, Camilo: *Priest and revolutionary, political programme and messages to the Colombian people*, London: 1968

Veliz, Claudio ed., *Obstacles to Change in Latin America*, London, 1969 *Latin America and the Caribbean, a handbook* London, 1968

Wheelock Román, Jaime *Imperialismo y dictadura*. Mexico: 1975

NOTES

PREFACE

[1]Jon Sobrino, inteview with the author, San Salvador, March 28, 1980.

[2]*The Revolt of Tonio Vasquez* was a radio programme broadcast by Radio Telefís Éireann in July 1980. Produced by Dr Donal Flanagan, the programme was based on recordings I made in Salvador.

CHAPTER ONE

[1]Entrance hymn from the Misa Campesina by Carlos Mejia Godoy. Describing the composition, he said: "It is not a neutral Mass. It is a Mass against the oppressor, against all those who prevent a share in the land."

[2]International Labour Organisation report quoted in *Human Rights in El Salvador*; a Report of a British Parliamentary Delegation in December, 1978, p.16.

[3]Report by Irish Franciscans, Gotera. Also Segundo Montes, *El Compadrazgo* (San Salvador, 1979), p.18.

[4]*ibid.*

[5]*ibid.*

[6]*ibid.*

[7]*Violence and Fraud in El Salvador,* compiled by the Latin American Bureau, July 1977, p.3.

[8]*ibid.*

[9]For general background, see Alistair White, *El Salvador* (London, 1973); David Browning, El Salvador, *Landscape and Society* (Oxford,1979).

[10]Everett Alan Wilson, "La Crisis de Integración national en El Salvador", in Rafael Manjivar and Rafael Guidos Véjar (eds.), *El Salvador de 1840 a 1939* (San Salvador, 1978), p.156. By 1919, 170,000 acres were either used for the production of coffee or designated to be cleared for the crop; by 1930, the number had risen to 260,000 acres.

[11]D. J. Rodgers to Sir John Simon, Jan. 7, 1932. FO 371/15812 XC/A/5313. Mr Rodgers referred to the same problem in reports on Jan. 13 and Feb. 12.

[12]*ibid.*

[13]D. J. Rodgers to Sir John Simon, Jan. 13, 1932. FO 371/15813 XC/A/5313.

[14]*ibid.*

¹⁵Arthur Harris to the US Department of Defence, December 22, 1931, United States Departmental Documents, National Archives, RG 59 810.00/828 quoted in Thomas Anderson, *El Salvador,* 1932 (Costa Rica, 1976) sp. ed., pp.129–130. The writer has translated the document, presumably originally written in English, from the Spanish translation of Thomas Anderson. The latter also noted that another American source reported that the largest landowner in Salvador, Miguel Dueno only paid $5,000 a year in taxes when he was obliged to pay about ten times that amount, p.149.

¹⁶The British envoy reported on December 19, 1931, that "general satisfaction" was being expressed that Aranjo had been ousted; he had disappointed not only the extravagant hopes aroused by the election campaign, but also the reasonable expectations of people in general." During his short tenure the floating debt had been doubled, ministers were incompetent and the 'spoils system' was in operation. Army pay was four months in arrears and there was a danger that Salvador might default on her Foreign Loan repayments. Aranjo had contemplated making a stand in Santa Tecla after escaping through a barracks window in the capital when the revolt broke out. Wiser counsel prevailed and he went into exile. A military directorate took over with Martinez as leader and on December 5, the *Diario Oficial* addressed Salvadorean citizens: "The edifice of the Nation is half in ruins. We are all going to rebuild it. We shall direct the work. You will give your vigorous cooperation." The military had come to power. Curiously, Rodgers laid great stress on the constitutional nature of the revolt. He had taken legal advice and found that to be true in the strictest sense. "The evil precedent will remain on record for the encouragement of other malcontents," he warned. At the Foreign Office D. V. Kelly minuted that the constitutional position of the government "illustrated the wisdom of giving as far as possible the benefit of the doubt to every de facto administration in South Central America. Practical conditions were much the most valuable guide." The Americans were forced to take a different view because of the 1923 treaty which pledged to withhold recognition from governments seizing power through force in any of the isthmian republics. See Kenneth J. Brieb, "The United States and the Rise of General Maximiliano Hernandez Martinez" in *Latin American Studies,* 3, 2, 151–172.

¹⁷Rodgers to Sir John Simon, January 22, 1932, FO 371/15813 XC/A/5313.

¹⁸Montes, *op. cit.,* p.183, quoting Méndez, pp.175–180, 155–172, 135–152, 115–122, 23, 112 and 9–20.

¹⁹D. J. Rodgers to Sir John Simon, February 12, 1932, FO 371/15813, XC/A/5313(189).

²⁰Rodgers, *loc. cit.*

²¹In Salvador I was told that the massacres of 1932 had been understated even by those partisan to the Indian cause.

²²Rodolfo Cardenal Chamorro, *Historia de la Iglesia de El Salvador,* San Salvador, 1976, manuscript quoted by Montes, *op. cit.*

[23] Anderson, *op. cit.*, p.198.

[24] D. J. Rodgers to Sir John Simon, January 22, 1932, FO 371/15813 XC/A/5313.

[25] D. J. Rodgers to Sir John Simon, February 12, 1932,FO 371/15813 XC/A/5313.

[26] (FO 371/15813, XC/A/5313)

[27] *Historiographical note:* Documentation concerning the campesino repression of 1932 is, not surprisingly, very uninformative and, more often, inaccessible to researchers in San Salvador. The writer was more fortunate in the American and British archives. Perhaps some of the most complete accounts of aspects of the rising and massacres can be found in the review, *ABRA Revista del Departmento de Letras de la Universidad Centroamericano José Sineon Canas,* June 13, 1976. The most compact account of the events of January 1932 can be found in Segundo Montes, *El Compadrazgo, op. cit.* The writer agrees with Montes that Anderson's titles of "El Salvador's Communist Revolt" is quite misleading — campesino or even Indian revolt would be much more accurate. In that sense the degree of Communist involvement has been exaggerated. Firstly, the massacre was carried out as part of a Christian crusade against bolshevism. A number of authors have been far too swift to compound the contrived judgment of General Martinez and add credibility to the 'red' rationale. F. D. Parker, *The Central American Republics* (London, 1964), p.151, quoted in Browning, *op. cit.,* p.273, "underrates the scale of the movement and the complexity of its causes." Joaquin Mendez, a journalist who travelled around with the troops during the repression had also a sharp ideological view: see *Los sucesos comunistas en El Salvador,* San Salvador, *1932.* Jorge Larde y Larin, *El Salvador: Historia de sus pueblos, villas y ciudades,* San Salvador, *1957,* fits into the same genre. As does Jorge Schlesesinger, *Revolucion Comunista: Guatemala en Peligro . . .?* Guatemala 1946. There are also a number of works sympathetic to the communist party which in turn over-state the impact of the central revolutionary leadership on the campesinos. Anderson's book has been mentioned already. Cf. Miguel Mármol. *Los Sucesos de 1932 en El Salvador,* San Jóse, 1972.

[28] Cf. Marcel Niedergang, *The Twenty Latin Americas,* vol. 1, (London: 1971), pp.335–345; John Gerassi, *The Great Fear in Latin America* (New York, 1967), pp.179–181; Claudio Valez ed., *Latin America and the Caribbean, a handbook* (London, 1968), pp.188–193; British Parliamentary Delegation Report, op. cit., p.19; Thomas Anderson, *El Salvador 1932* (trans., Costa Rica, 1976); Eduardo Colindres, *Fundamentos Economicos de la Burguesia Salvadorena* (San Salvador 1977), and Edelberto Torres Rivas, *Interpretacion del Desarrollo Social Centroamericano* (Costa Rica, 1977).

[29] British Parliamentary Report, *op. cit.,* p.21.

[30] For an analysis of the associations and of recent political developments see the very informative articles in *ECA, Estudios Centroamericanos* published by the Catholic University, UCA, in San Salvador.

153

[31]The *campesinos* had been banned from organising since the suppression of the peasant revolt in 1932.

[32]Amnesty International sources would place the strength of ORDEN in the period even higher at between 80,000 and 100,000.

[33]*El Salvador, a country study* (Washington, 1979), p.195.

[34]*ibid.*

[35]Carlos Andino Martinez, "El Estamento Militar en el Salvador" *ECA,* July–August 1979, Nos. 369–370, pp.615–630. The article puts forward a very interesting thesis cited above relating to the qualitative change in military participation in politics, marked by the proclamation of January 25, 1961. There are also a series of very important tables (1) on the formation and payment of the armed forces; (2) pay of the various ranks from cabo with 130 escudos per month to a general who gets 2,500 escudos; (3, 4 & 5) the names and details of officers holding positions in the private sector, and military who served as ambassadors; (6) specialist courses for military abroad. Nicolas Mariscal, "Militares y Reformismo en El Salvdor", *ECA,* Jan.-Feb. 1978, n. 351/352, pp. 9-27.

[36]José Comblin, *The Church and the National Security State* (New York, 1979).

[37]*ibid.,*p.65.

[38]*ibid.,* p.74.

[39]José Comblin on the National Security Doctrine, *"Idoc International"* (new series), Bulletin no. 1–2, January–February, 1977, p.6. Cf. Theo Westow, "The Ideology of National Security", *New Blackfriars,* Vol. 61, n. 717, February 1980, pp.52–61.

[40]Thomas R. Campos, "La Seguridad Nacional y la Constitución Salvadorena", in *ECA,* July–August, 1979, nos. 369–370, pp.477–488; and Guillermo Manuel Ungo, "Los Derechos Humanos, Condicion Necesaria para la Paz y Convivencia Social en El Salvador," *ibid.,* pp.489–506; Dr. Ungo who has already been mentioned is the leader of the Salvadorean Social Democratic Party.

[41]The US Assistant Secretary of State for Inter-American Affairs, Mr. Viron P. Vaky, visited El Salvador at the end of July, following the flight of Somoza from Nicaragua. He told the US House of Representatives Committee on Inter-American Affairs in September that El Salvador was the most volatile country in Central America. It had a "classic setting for social and political unrest," and the "prospects for avoiding insurrectional violence was (sic) rapidly diminishing". He said that El Salvador had "one of the most rigid class structures" in the hemisphere, that there had been serious violations of human rights, and that the political system had been unable to accommodate dissent. It is quite clear that President Carter was anxious to replace President Romero with an administration capable of initiating political and social reform.

[42]Country reports on Human Rights Practices for 1979, submitted to both Senate and House of Representatives Committees on Foreign Relations, February 4, 1980, p.315.

154

[43]*Nicaragua, Dictatorship and Revolution,* Latin America Bureau special brief (London, 1979) and Eduardo Crawley, *Dictators never Die* (a portrait of Nicaragua and the Somozas) London, 1979

[44]*Economist,* February 23, 1980, p.18.

[45]Carolyn Forché, "Anatomy of Counter-Revolution: The Road to Reaction in El Salvador." *Nation,* June 14, 1980.

[46]*Keesing's Contemporary Archive* 30046, January 25, 1980, puts the casualties at 30, and quotes one source pushing the figure to 70. But according to contacts in Salvador, the figure was probably even higher.

[47]That name D'Abuisson has a chilling ring in Salvador where he is seen to be one of the main architects of right-wing violence. He was a national guard intelligence officer, in his late 30s, before being sacked by the October 15 junta. He tried to stage a coup in May, 1980, only to be arrested and imprisoned. His bid was said to have had the support of many wealthy businessmen and an undetermined sector of the military. As proof of his personal strength he was released from jail.

[48]The story of Fredy Antonio Vasquez was told to me in Salvador by some very dear friends who work tirelessly in the cause of human rights and social justice. They knew Tonio personally.

[49]Fredy Antonio Vásquez is listed in Amnesty reports as being detained and killed on January 25 by the national guard; he is described as a *jornalero,* a peasant day-labourer.

[50]This letter was sent to a priest and shown to the writer.

CHAPTER TWO

[1]The majority of foreign priests and religious working in Salvador were Italian and Spanish. But there are also North American missionaries from the diocese of Cleveland and a small community of Irish Franciscan and Saint Clare nuns working in the remote Gotera area near the Honduran Border.

[2]Anon., *Rutilio Grande* (San Salvador, 1978).

[3]Rutilio Grande, homily delivered at Apopa on the occasion of the expulsion of the parish priest Mario Bernal, *Orientacion,* March 27, 1977.

[4]Rutilio Grande Sermon, *op. cit.*

[5]*Orientacion,* March 27, 1977.

[6]*ibid.*

[7]On June 11, 1980, the *Irish Times* reported that a group of 16 Vincentian priests in Panama City had made public a letter they wrote to Bishop Alverez, who is a member of the same Order. They asked him to "resign immediately your rank as a Colonel in the Salvadorean Army" and "to make a profound examination of conscience with the help of the Gospel, the Documents of the Second Vatican Council and the writings of Archbishop Romero."

155

They urged the bishop to follow the example of other Latin American bishops who have supported the struggles of the poor and "go ask pardon of the Salvadorean people for your failings as a fellow Christian and as their pastor."

The letter came a day after San Salvador's apostolic administrator, Monsignor Arturo Rivera Damas, said 2,056 people had been killed in political violence that year and advised Salvadoreans to store food to prepare for future "difficulties."

In his response, Bishop Alvarez thanked the priests for their letter but declined to take up any of the points made. According to *The Tablet* he said: "It is sufficient for me at this moment to re-read the opening address of our Holy Father Pope John Paul II, during the Third General Asembly of Latin American Bishops, which took place in Puebla, especially Part III, No, 1ff."

[8]Ronald Cueto Ruiz, "Thoughts on Bartolomé de las Casas OP", *New Blackfriars,* Vol. 56, No. 664, September 1975, p.409.

[9]"La Iglesia y las Organisaziones Politicas Populares" (San Salvador, 1978), trans. "The Church, Political Organisation and Violence", 1980, sponsored by CIIR, CAFOD and Trócaire.

[10]Declaration of the El Salvadorean Episcopate about some popular political organisations, issued on August 28, 1978: the document was signed by Pedro Arnoldo Aparicio y Quanitanilla, Jose Eduardo Alvarez, Benjamin Barrera y Reyes, bishop of Santa Ana, Marco Rene Revelo, auxiliary of San Salvador and Freddy Delgado,

[11]James, 2: 15–16.

[12]On the Development of Peoples, No. 24.

[13]Helder Camara, *Race against Time* (London, 1971), pp.78–79.

[14]Jon Sobrino, "The significance of Puebla for the Catholic Church in Latin America", in *Reflections on Puebla* (London, 1980), pp.23–23.

[15]Sobrino, *op. cit.,* pp.22–23

[16]*ibid.,* p.22

[17]See interview with Bishop Jose Eduardo Alvarez in Radharc film "Who is for Liberation?" It is certainly true that Romero was very friendly with Jon Sobrino and Ignacio Ellacuria — both highly-respected theologians who live in Salvador. But the archbishop was very much his own man. See also "Los Jesuitas ante el Pueblo Salvadoreno" (San Salvador, 1977).

[18]*Violence and Fraud in El Salvador,* pp.20–27.

[19]See Jim O'Halloran, *Living Cells, Building Basic Christian Community,* Dominican Publications, Dublin, 1980

[20]The Provincial of the Irish Franciscans, Fr. David O'Reilly, and the Mother Superior of the Order of St. Clare, Sr. Helen Conway, wrote to the Irish nuncio Mgr. Alibrandi on requesting him "To convey to His Holiness, Pope John Paul II, our deep concern over the present state of affairs in El Salvador and the apparent Vatican support of the repressive junta by the known attitude of the Papal Nuncio in Salvador." The nuncio was recalled from El Salvador in April, 1980.

[21]*La Opinion,* September, 1978.

[22]Cartoon cutting in Franciscan archive, Gotera.

[23]Rutilio Grande sermon, *Orientación,* March 27, 1977: intimidation of catechists is now a commonplace in the country.

[24]*El Diario de Hoy,* August 14, 1978 and August 7, 1980.

[25]*Mission de la Iglesia en Medio de la Crisis del Pais,* August, 1979, p.30.

[26]*op. cit.,* p.64.

CHAPTER THREE

[1]*Orientación,* May 22, 1977; also *Justicia y Paz,* May 1977, No. 65.

[2]*ibid.*

[3]Franciscan archive, Gotera. Other names were Caballeros de Cristo Rey; Asociacion de Seguidores de Cristo Rey; Cruzados Catolicos; Consejo Coordinador nacional de Faro; Comite pro mejoramiento de la Iglesia Catolica; Sociedad de Mujeres Cristianas; Asociacion de Mujeres Religiosas Catolicas; Fieles Catolicos Salvadorenos.

[4]Interview with Rivera Damas.

[5]Clerical source in Salvador.

[6]*Orientación,* January 28, 1979: In the cathedral of San Salvador, on March 30, the writer was introduced to the parents of Father Octavio Ortiz just before bombs went off. They were from Cacoapera in Morazan. From another source the writer learned that Father Ortiz could not get permission from the local bishop to celebrate Mass in his home town. The man in question was Bishop Alvarez who has been mentioned a number of times in the text. Fr. Ortiz had begun to study for that diocese and had changed to the capital where he was befriended by Romero. Bad relations between the young priest and the bishop dated from that time. However, thanks to local help, Fr. Ortiz did say Mass in his home village.

[7]Excerpts from Romero questionnaire in *IDOC International,* new series, Bulletin No. 6 and 7, June–July 1978, pp.3–7.

[8]Puebla is treated in detail elsewhere. See Austin Flannery, "From Medellin to Puebla" in *Doctrine and Life,* March–April, 1979, p.205. Julian Filochowski, "Medellin to Puebla", *Reflections on Puebla* (London, 1980), pp.15–16. Three views of Puebla can be found in the *Spectator,* see: Peter Hebblethwaite, "The Divided Church", *Spectator,* January 27, 1979, for a crisp introduction to the background of the conference. Peter Nichols "The Paradoxes at Puebla", *Spectator,* February 17, 1980, is a rather good critique of the proceedings which stands in marked contrast to the article by Edward Norman, "Confronting the Radicals" in the same issue.

[9]See Puebla documents.

[10]Jon Sobrino interview.

[11]Romero had gone on *ad limina* visit to Rome in 1978 where he met Pope Paul VI and explained the situation in his country to a man who had studied the country in some considerable detail

[12]*Orientación,* February 24, 1980: Trócaire, the Catholic Development Agency in Ireland, had helped fund the diocesan newspaper, the radio station and the human rights commission set up by Romero.

[13]*Orientación,* March 30, 1980.

[14]Private sources in Salvador consulted in March and substantiated by other sources in recent months.

CHAPTER FOUR

[1]*Times,* March 26, 1980: page 1 report on the killing. Mgr. Urioste told the writer a different version in an interview from Salvador by phone on March 26 and later in the country. He spoke of one shot fired by a man who was possibly an expert.

[2]Rivera Damas interview.

[3]*Times,* March 26, 1980.

[4]*Times,* March 26, 1980.

[5]*Orientación,* March 30, 1980.

[6]*El Diario de Hoy,* March 31,1980.

[7]The letter was signed by Bishops Sergio Mendez Arceo, Mexico; Samuel Ruiz, Mexico; Leonidas Proano, Ecuador; Jacques Menager, France; Luciano Mendez, Brazil; Luis A Bambaren, Peru; Marcus McGrath, Panama; Eamon Casey, Ireland; James O'Brien; England; by Dr. Charles Harper, World Council of Churches; Dr. Angel V. Peiro, ibid.; Jose Antonio Perez, ibid,; Doctor Joyce Lara Braun, ibid,; Dr. Victor Mercado, ibid.; by Fathers Juan Vives, Venezuela; Luis Maria Coinochea, Peru; Gustavo Gutierrez, Peru; Simon Smith, America; Gerard Dupond, Brazil; by Sisters Regina McEroy, USA; Josephine Caller, ibid.; and Maria Moore, ibid.

[8]Private source who witnessed the exchange.

[9]*La Prensa Grafica.* April 1, 1980, published the sermon.

[10]Private source.

[11]*El Diario de Hoy,* April 2, 1980.

[12]*La Prensa Grafica,* April 1, 1980.

[13]Archbishop John R. Quinn of San Francisco, statement, April 7, 1980.

CHAPTER FIVE

[1]Keesing's contemporary archives, 29020, June 9, 1978: Chamorro (53), who has been referred to earlier, was a prominent member of the official Guatemalan opposition conservative party (PCN) and leader of the unofficial opposition Democratic Liberation Union

(UDEL). He was editor of *La Prensa* — one of the most important papers in Latin America. Sr. Chamorro was imprisioned several times and spent three periods in exile for opposition activities.

[2]Jon Sobrino, interview with author, March 28, 1980, San Salvador.

[3]Louvain address, published in Spanish in *Mensaje* (Chile), No. 288, May, 1980.

[4]Sobrino interview.

[5]Louvain address.

[6]The source quoted above is *Gist,* El Salvador US Policy, March 1980, Bureau of Public Affairs, Department of State, Washington. In view of the continued Salvadorean armed forces' involvement in repression, Cardinal Ó Fiaich and Bishop Eamon Casey have written requesting a halt in flow of military credits. So also did six English bishops.

[7]Charles E. Rushing, US Embassy, Dublin, to Brendan Butler, chairman of the El Salvador Support Committee, April 23, 1980

[8]Cesar Jerez, The Mission of the Society of Jesus To-day and Our Common Struggle for Justice, speech delivered at Canisius College, 1978.

[9]General background to Guatemala, read: Thomas and Marjorie Melville, *Guatemala — another Vietnam?* (London, 1971) and Eduardo Galeano, *Guatemala: Occupied Country* (London, 1977).

[10]Jerez speech, *loc. cit.*

[11]Francisco Andres Escobar, *Peticion y Ofrenda* (San Salvador, 1979), pp.53-57.

[12]Statement found in *ECA,* n.380, June, 1980, pp. 597-598 and 635-636.

EPILOGUE

[1]*Mondo* (A San Salvador evening paper) reported the arrest by police in the early evening edition. See *El Pais,* Madrid, 29 November, 1980.

[2]I met Juan Chacon at a press conference at the UCA, the Catholic University, on 29 March, 1980. Following the violence in the cathedral I met him again in the archbishop's palace, He was a participant in the meeting of visiting foreign bishops. There I had the opportunity of a long conversation with him.

[3]*El Pais,* 29 November 1980.

[4]I have been on that road quite a number of times, but only once at night. On that occasion we passed a military patrol on the way to the airport, and saw at least two on the return trip. Cars and lorries are stopped as a matter of course during the day by patrols.

[5]*Times,* London, 9 and 11 December, 1980.

[6]*ibid.,* 11 December, 1980.

[7]*ibid.* Cordova and Majano remained close friends despite the fact that the former headed the clandestine FDR and the latter remained

in the junta. Majano had maintained that the FDR should be invited
to join in any peace negotiations that might occur.

[8]While he was in Britain in November, 1980, Dr Ruben Zamora,
who was a secretary to the first junta, and who is now in exile in
Mexico, told me of this incident. He said the other members of the
junta were shocked.